# Glory at Ground Level

Prayer Handbook Advent 2005-2006

**Contributors**
Barbara Bennett, Ken Chippindale, Carla Grosch-Miller,
Jasmine Jebakani, David Jonathan, Deborah McVey,
Helen Pope, Heather Whyte, Brian Woodcock.

**Editor**
Ken Chippindale

# FOREWORD

When Jesus was born and lived in Galilee and Judea some 2000 years ago, he came to bring an awareness of who God is within the grasp of ordinary people. It is in that sense that our title, 'Glory at Ground Level', taken from Brian Woodcock's Maundy Thursday prayer, is to be understood. To put it another way, in and through the Incarnation of Jesus the glory of God is made known in the world.

I hope that you will let your imagination play with that image as you use the contents of this Prayer Handbook. Our writers do not claim to be expert pray-ers – which of us could say that? Rather do they offer the way their own thoughts have been led by one or more of the bible passages set for a particular Sunday. Maybe one phrase or emphasis will lead you down a path you have not been before. Two of our writers are from India; so inevitably their approach, arising from another culture and written in their second language, will be different.

I find it interesting that the Latin word, from which we get 'humble' and 'humiliation', is 'humus', meaning 'ground 'or 'earth'. Jesus shared our human life in humility (Philippians 2:8). He lived at ground level amongst the earthy peasants of Galilee. His ministry was in the midst of the political and social pressures facing an occupied country. He dealt with the everyday concerns of people who were disabled or ill, touching them to heal and to bless. He ate alongside the respectable and disreputable alike. Through this human life, humbly lived, the glory of God shone, and still shines (2 Corinthians 4:6).

Alongside these prayers are stories and reflections, from around the world, of how that glory is seen in our world today. They come from the ground level of ordinary life, which sometimes is the ground zero of a 9/11 or a tsunami wave. Even there – some would say especially there – we can glimpse the glory of God, at work in human compassion and in sacrificial giving and service.

I wish to record my grateful thanks to this year's contributors; Barbara Bennett, minister at Ilfracombe; Carla Grosch-Miller, ordained by the United Church of Christ in the USA, and now serving in the URC; Jasmine Jebakani, from the Church of South India and currently studying for a PhD at Manchester University; David Jonathan, from the Church of North India, currently working with different faith communities in a project partnership between CWM, the URC and the Grassroots programme in Luton; Deborah McVey, Chaplain to the East Anglian Ministerial Training Course and at Addenbrooke's Hospital, Cambridge; Helen Pope, minister at Dawlish; and Brian Woodcock, a former Warden of Iona Abbey, and minister at Trinity, St Albans and Bricket Wood. Jasmine worked as a theological educator at the Southern Theological Education and Training scheme from 1999-2003, and Carla is currently on the academic staff there. I would also like to thank the Editorial Board for their work, under the convenorship of Debbie Martin of the Congregational Federation.

This volume brings to an end my stint as editor, and I would like to especially mention my thanks to Wendy Cooper in Church House for her unfailing helpfulness and efficiency, which makes the production of the Handbook possible; and also Sara Foyle for her creative input. I have been grateful for this opportunity to serve the church, and I hope that this Handbook will be an aid to our closer walk with God in the pilgrimage of our lives.

*Ken Chippindale*

# Prayers for Seven Days

These are primarily based on the widely accepted FIVE MARKS OF MISSION.
You are invited to arrange a symbol, representing the theme of that day, as you begin. If you are using the prayers each week, you are invited to select one point from each section on which to focus.

## SUNDAY – WORSHIP
*symbol: a lighted candle, fragrant if possible.*

"The United Reformed Church acknowledges its responsibility under God: to make its life a continual offering of itself and the world to God in adoration and worship through Jesus Christ'.
*(United Reformed Church Basis of Union)*

"The chief end of man is to worship God and enjoy him forever'.
*(Westminster Shorter Confession)*

Before all else, as we begin this day and this week, we give our worship to you, ever-present and ever-loving God. Even if we cannot do anything else, as individuals or as a church, we bring to you our sincere praise. With grateful hearts, as we recollect the blessings of this past week, we offer you our adoration.

Forgive us when we get so caught up in the worries and anxieties, the rush and pressures, of everyday life that we forget to worship you.
Forgive us when we allow our priorities to be dictated by the world's agenda, and we push worship to the periphery of life, squeezed in or left out.
Forgive us when our worship becomes routine, a duty instead of a delight; when we hear without understanding and speak without feeling.
Forgive us when the worthy but lesser things intrude on what is fundamental in the life of our church, and we put more effort into the annual fete or weekly coffee morning than our Sunday services.

Pray for all those in your, and every, church who will be preparing for public worship, however large or small a part they play. Ask that each one, as you visualise them in your church, will devote themselves wholeheartedly to the task in hand, and do it for God and his glory and not for their own gratification.

Pray for all those who will be coming to church today – longstanding members and newcomers, young and old; for those who will be coming from the hubbub of family homes and those who spend most of their time on their own; for those who will be coming to seek answers and for those who are certain; for those who are at their wits end with anxiety or pain, and those whose lives are comfortable and content.

Pray for those who will not be in church today – for the frail older person; for any who are sick, at home or in hospital, and those caring for them; for those visiting relatives or away on holiday; for those who have to work, even thought they would rather be in church; for those harbouring a grievance; for those whose faith is going through a crisis.

*Give thanks for:*

*all preachers, who have struggled with scripture in order to make God's word meaningful and relevant to the congregation today;*

*all who have the responsibility of leading prayers, thinking also of those who have written prayers for public use, seeking to use language creatively;*

*those who lead the music of the church, recognising how important this is within the whole of worship; for organists and pianists, for choirs and soloists, for bands and instrumentalists;*

*for all who have the gift of composing church music, both classical and modern;*

*for those whose artistic gifts enhance our worship – in dance and movement, banner making, and flower arranging;*

*for architects and builders, constructing the new, or adapting the old, so that our places of worship might reflect our contemporary understanding of worship and church.*

## MONDAY – TELL
### *To proclaim the good news of the Kingdom*
*symbol: an open Bible*

Monday morning: back to work, back to the everyday routine, the ordinary round, the world of office and factory and shop, the so-called secular world.

Lord of all the world, creator of all that is, we praise you for the whole of human endeavour, for science and technology and business and commerce, and all that contributes to human wellbeing.

Help us to see that this is where the good news needs to be spoken and known; where the values of the market place need to be challenged by the values of the kingdom; where the blind forces of globalisation should know the will of the creator; and where the life of Christ can be experienced in the actions of every Christian.

Forgive us if we have forsaken the secular world, leaving it bereft of the Good News of the kingdom.

Forgive us if, because of shyness or diffidence, or the fear of imposing our beliefs on others, we have kept our faith private.

Forgive us if, because of being thought different, we have not spoken up for a more Christian way.

Forgive us if, because we have not felt sure enough about our faith, we have not offered spiritual help to someone in need.

Forgive us if, because we have spent so much of our time and effort in churchly things, we have lost contact with the world outside.

Father, forgive us and help us.

Think of those who passed on the good news to you. Give thanks for parents, Sunday school teachers, ministers, friends; recognising with hindsight those who were faithful in this, even though you were not ready to listen.

Pray for those known to you who will be seeking to do this now – parents with their children; Junior church staff, faced with sporadic attendance and so many counter attractions; ministers, amidst the varied responsibilities laid upon them; friends, who want to say the right thing at the right time.

Pray that each will be given the spirit of perseverance, and might offer themselves as a channel for the work of the Holy Spirit.

Think of those known to you who seem to be untouched by the good news – those whose behaviour and lifestyle you deplore;

those you see regularly and feel are searching for something in their lives; maybe people who are celebrities and role models; maybe your own family and friends. Pray for them now, asking that God will make himself known in their lives.

*Pray for:*
*all called to a specific ministry of evangelism;*
*those who produce courses, like Alpha and Emmaus, to make the Good News accessible;*
*those using such courses in prisons, in the workplace and with young people;*
*all chaplains – in schools, hospitals and universities, to industry and shopping centres;*
*all biblical scholars and teachers in theological colleges;*
*all work-based, school and college Christian groups;*
*all Missions planned for 2006;*
*all Christians with power to influence others, because of their celebrity status, in sport or show-business, politics or business.*

## TUESDAY – TEACH
### To teach, baptise, and nurture new believers
*symbol: a glass of water*

Thank God for all who are becoming Christian world-wide;
may they remain faithful.
Give glory to God for the possibilities of growth in the faith;
may they never cease.
Praise God for the commitments entered into at baptism;
may they be kept.

Forgive us, Lord, if we have become lukewarm in our response to your love, and if we have doubted the sincerity of others when they have made promises.
Forgive us, if we have become unwilling to change in matters of faith, and if we have stood in the way of others desiring to know more about you.
Forgive us if we have created a clique of those we get on with in church, and if therefore we have made others feel excluded.

Renew and empower us by the Holy Spirit, that our eyes may be open to new truth, and be enabled to see the next steps of our pilgrimage unfold. As we journey out into a new landscape of faith enable us to help our fellow travellers, whatever speed they may be going. Grant us the grace to assist those moving slowly, and keep us from envy of those far ahead of us. Above all keep us from the temptation of spiritual pride, thinking that *I* know, and *they* don't.

Think of those who have been baptised or received into membership in your church in the last year (if necessary, obtain a list from your church secretary). Pray for them by name over the course of a month. Think also of those who have taken a new step of faith. Pray for new elders, for those joining a house group for the first time, for people on TLS courses for lay training and lay preachers (or their equivalent in each denomination), for those candidating for the ministry.

*Pray for:*
> *ministers meeting parents who want their children baptised or blessed;*
> *all house group or study group leaders;*
> *those leading, and those taking, Church membership courses;*
> *District, Synod, and National staff who facilitate training events and courses;*
> *people who are commissioned to produce material to nurture growth in faith;*
> *those whose gift is to welcome people into church and offer friendship;*
> *all the community of the church, in which each has a responsibility to show love and care for any who want to belong.*

## WEDNESDAY – TEND
### *To respond to human need by loving service*
symbol: a towel (Mark 10:45)

We give thanks, loving God, that you have shown your true nature in the life, death and resurrection of Jesus Christ, and that at the heart of this is the knowledge that you are love. We thank you that Jesus grounded his ministry in acts of loving service; love in the form of acceptance, healing, reconciliation and forgiveness; service by accepting the role of the slave. We praise you that we have this clear picture as to how we are to be as Christian people.

Forgive us when we suffer compassion fatigue because of the enormity of human need, and so do not respond to any situation.
Forgive us if we have not responded because we were too wrapped up in our own or our family's life, and thereby turned our backs on others.
Forgive us when we have thought ourselves above some acts of service,

either because the person needing help or the task required to be done, we found unpleasant.

Forgive us when, forgetting how lucky we are in comparison with so many places in the world, we have kept our material blessings to ourselves.

Lord, as you open our eyes to Jesus, so open our eyes equally to the needs of others. Help us to see him, in them (Matthew 25:40). Grant us the awareness to see where we can best respond, sensitively, appropriately, and with the servant spirit of Jesus.

> Think of a person you know who is in some kind of need.
> Think of a situation in your community (town, city) where there is need also.
> Spend some time praying for these people and situations.
>
> Pray that there may be a swift response to the need.
> Is there anything you personally, or your church, could do?
> Ask to be led, maybe in some new way, to offer the unconditional love of Christ.

*Pray for particular charities and organisations working in the field of social service especially known to you, including:*

> *Church Action against Poverty;*
> *Shelter;*
> *Telephone Samaritans;*
> *Alcoholics Anonymous, Al-Anon, Drug Advice and Rehabilitation schemes;*
> *Charities known to you which help children, including Childline;*
> *Front line workers in the meeting of need – Social workers, Probation officers, Teachers, Doctors, Nurses …*

## THURSDAY – TRANSFORM
### *To seek to transform the unjust structures of society*
symbol: white wrist band (Make Poverty History), or red ribbon
(Trade Justice movement), or Commitment for Life envelope

We praise you, Loving God, that you have created our world and sustain it in being, giving us in Jesus the model, both for our lives and for all human institutions. We thank you that Jesus came to bring good news to the poor, liberty to captives, recovery of sight to the blind, and freedom to the oppressed (Luke 4:18-20). We remember all the ways in which these promises have been fulfilled over the ages, throughout the world, and that today there are universal values, which are generally recognised.

Forgive us, we pray, when we are complicit in keeping unjust situations in place, be they unfair trade agreements, or institutions which favour the rich and discriminate against the poor.
Have mercy on us if we have voted in elections simply to preserve our self-interest, instead of considering the common good.
Forgive us if we have allowed prejudice or biased media coverage to shape our views, which, when put into practice, cause suffering to the innocent.
Have mercy on us if we have simply shut our minds and hearts to the plight of people at the other side of the world.

Think of one situation at present in the news which is an 'unjust structure': this might be a story about a farmer in Ghana, or an asylum seeker from Zimbabwe, or a forthcoming world economic summit.
Pray for all the people concerned with that situation, both the 'victims', and those with power. Remember also those dealing with the situation at 'ground level', who are required to obey orders – police, government officials, company employees.
Pray too for all those who are trying to uncover, publicise, and challenge injustices, often putting themselves at risk.
Think of those who have made known the story on which you are focusing.
Pray for yourself, that you may be shown the way in which you could make a difference to a situation of injustice in the world.

*Pray for:*
> *the Make Poverty History campaign;*
> *the Trade Justice movement, and Traidcraft;*
> *our Commitment for Life partners;*
> *the work of Christian Aid, Tearfund, and other development agencies;*
> *leaders of governments, finance ministers, World Bank and IMF*
> *officials, and all with power to change policy.*

## FRIDAY – TREASURE
*To strive to safeguard the integrity of creation,*
*to sustain and renew the life of the earth*
*symbol: something natural (eg a flower from your garden or a pot plant,*
*a piece of bark, a stone even)*

Praise be to God for all the wonders of creation; for the
incomprehensible vastness of space, the millions of stars and planets,
the sheer miracle of the exactitude of all the factors which make the
existence of life possible on this fragile blue, green and white ball.
Praise be to God for the harmony and balance in our world; for
the tilt of the Earth at just the right angle; for the exact mix of the
various chemicals; for the life-giving flow of the ocean currents; for
the necessary cycle of cloud and wind and rain and sun, and the
predictability of the seasons.
Praise be to God for the countless species in the world; for those we
know about and have classified, and those we have yet to discover;
for the immense variety of animals and insects, birds, fish and plants,
in all their different appearances of size and shape and colour.
Praise be to God for humankind; for the wonder of our evolution and
development; for the intricacy and complexity and balance of the
human body; for the growth of moral reasoning and ethical values; for
our dawning sense of responsibility for this planet and the realisation
that we hold its future in our hands.

Creator God, forgive us when we have lived as if the planet had a
limitless supply for all our needs and desires.
Forgive us when, being made aware of the dangers of global warming,
excessive consumption and pollution, we have not altered our lifestyle
appropriately.
Forgive us if we have simply shut our minds to the problems,
impervious to the bitter legacy we will be leaving to our children and
grandchildren.
Lord, in granting us your forgiveness, make us aware of our immediate
responsibility to change the way we live, and lead us to know both
what we should do and cease from doing.

Think of a local scheme which exists to play a part in the restoring of the right balance in the natural world. This might be a re-cycling service, a conservation group, an action group trying to persuade people to do things differently (e.g. give up 4x4 cars and air travel, cycle more, use the train). Pray for the success of that scheme, and that its influence might grow.
Pray for the work in schools so that a new generation will not make the mistakes of the past.
Think of any recent item in the news, either local or international, which illustrates these issues, and pray for all concerned with that problem.

*Pray for:*
   *those affected by thoughtless and careless use of the environment;*
   *people living in the shadow of smoke and fumes from unregulated*
   *factories in Eastern Europe and the developing world;*
   *all environmental agencies in this country and throughout the world;*
   *all charities like Greenpeace and Friends of the Earth;*
   *those groups which seek to preserve the natural habitat, e.g. RSPB,*
   *the Woodland Trust;*
   *world leaders, that they might make environmental issues of the*
   *highest priority;*
   *church bodies, like Eco-congregation, which challenge us;*
   *scientists who are giving us early warning of the consequences, and*
   *therefore enabling us to avoid impending disaster.*

## SATURDAY – CREATE
### *To offer all human creativity in the service of God*
*symbol: something you have made, or which represents a hobby, or skill you possess*

Creative and creating God, we praise you that you have made every human being in your image, reflecting your creativity. We rejoice in the diversity of humanity in all its richness, with its many colours, racial characteristics, languages and cultural patterns. Help us to give thanks for our neighbours in the global village, though they be different from us; may we treasure what they have to teach us.

Forgive us when we have succumbed to the temptation to fear those who are different from us, and allowed that fear to turn to suspicion or antagonism.

Forgive us when we have been envious of others, those who can do so easily and well what we struggle to do badly.

Forgive us if we have neglected to bring to fruition the gifts you have given us, allowing them to remain dormant and unused.

Forgive us if we have used our gifts in proud and arrogant ways, making others feel their contribution to be of little value.

Help us, we pray, to offer all that you have given us, both our innate talents and abilities, and what we have received through the Holy Spirit, to you. May every person be enabled to bring their gifts to full potential, and use them appropriately, for the greater good and your delight.

Think of a gift you have been given – artistic, musical, intellectual (using words and ideas), practical (making or mending things, cooking, sewing), social skills (conversing easily, making friends, giving hospitality), organising or leading.

Thank God for it, and ask how it might be more fully used, or be developed further.

Ask God that you be given the gifts of the Holy Spirit for the building up of the church.

Think of someone you know, and ask that they might be affirmed in the use or development of their gifts, for their own well-being and for the health of the whole church.

*Pray for all, who through the use of their creativity can open new worlds to us:*

> *musicians and composers;*
> *painters and sculptors;*
> *actors, directors and film makers;*
> *gardeners and horticulturalists;*
> *naturalists and wildlife experts;*
> *workers in tapestry and weaving;*
> *cooks and culinary experts;*
> *mechanics, and wood and metal workers;*
> *writers, novelists and poets;*
> *adult education and language teachers.*

Isaiah 64:1-9
Psalm 80:1-7, 17-19
1 Corinthians 1:3-9
Mark 13:24-37

## World AIDS Day – 1 December

Ashar Alo means 'light of hope'. It was started by the Christian Commission for Development in Bangladesh in 1991, and is now an independent society, providing support to people with HIV/AIDS in Dhaka and two other centres. There is much discrimination shown against those living with HIV/AIDS: most hospitals refuse them treatment and they are excluded from their families.

Since women usually live with their husband's families, they are treated as outcastes when it is discovered they are HIV positive. At the same time, they are blamed for their condition, even if is their husband who has infected them, which is usually the case.

In neighbouring India, the church has put huge resources into building a massive healthcare service that is making a powerful contribution to the anti-AIDS campaign. It is estimated that the current number infected there is 5.1 million, but some agencies say that 25 million Indians will be infected by 2010.

Meanwhile, in Botswana an annual government-backed beauty pageant for HIV-positive women is helping to combat AIDS. They demonstrate their poise and grace in evening wear, and perform traditional dance, as well as speaking about HIV/AIDS. The winner of the title Miss HIV Stigma Free teaches others about the importance of testing for the virus, and teaching them how to live positively with the illness.

Also the UN has praised a 2004 Bollywood movie for its attempt to break the ignorance and stigma surrounding the disease, when the star of the film is seen suffering from AIDS.

**Tender God, in whose arms all people are loved,
we bring our prayers for all who live with HIV/AIDS.
To children who have been orphaned, be a guardian;
to grandparents who have taken in new families, be a strength;
to carers who seek to put an end to stigma, be an inspiration;
and to all of us, as we seek an end to this terrible virus,
be a teacher and a guide, and an everlasting hope.**

Anxious eyes scan the skies,
from whence will our help come, O Lord?

The world teeters on the brink of madness.
Terror has made a home among us.
Your name is inscribed on bullets and bombs
 dealing death and destruction, desecrating life made in your image.
Children bear the scars of knife wounds inflicted by other children.
      No place is safe, no person immune
      from the virus of violence that has taken hold of our world.

You have made a world of plenty and of beauty,
 a world where there is more than enough for all.
Yet enough is not in our vocabulary.
Our greed and insecurity drive us incessantly toward more.
The earth bears the scars of the rapacious appetites of her children.
      No continent is left untouched, no human endeavour unsullied
      by the ravages of short-sighted selfishness.

Can you not, will you not, stir up your might and come to save us?
Can you not, will you not, tear open heavens and make nations tremble?

We are waiting, Lord.
Without you, we are unable to make the peace for which we long.
Without you, we are captive to the worst in ourselves.
Without you, we have no hope.

We hurl our prayers into your silence,
waiting for you, whose vulnerability will tease out our tenderness;
you, for whom the darkness holds no threat;
you, who will set all things aright as you make a home in our hearts.
We wait for you.

## God is still speaking

*'Never place a period where God has placed a comma' – Gracie Allen*

The advertising campaign used by the United Church of Christ in the run up to Christmas 2004 had a far wider impact than the writers of the advert could have imagined. The Wisconsin Conference of the UCC has had a partnership arrangement with the South Western Synod for many years and it was during a courtesy visit to the Conference Minister that I was made aware of how important the campaign had become. As part of a nationwide campaign the UCC had paid for an advert to be screened on television to promote the message that everyone is welcome within the UCC. The short commercial begins with two nightclub 'bouncers' controlling who has access to a church. Two young men holding hands approach and are turned away with the words *'No, step aside please'*. They are followed by a young Hispanic man who is stopped with the words *'No way,'* and an African American woman with the put down *'I don't think so'*. In between white middle class couples are let through without challenge. The ad ends with the words *'Jesus didn't turn people away, neither do we'*.

The commercial was considered so controversial that two major broadcasting companies, CBS and NBC, withdrew the agreement to screen on the eve of the broadcast. The resulting publicity ensured that the ad was reported on by news channels and in the press, resulting in far more people seeing or at least hearing of the campaign than might otherwise have been reached by the straightforward commercial.

What struck me was the way in which the controversy, far from cowing the members of the UCC, had given them fresh impetus and a greater determination to get the message across that *'no matter who you are or where you are on life's journey, you're welcome here'*. The message is unambiguous, they are confident in telling it and their self-belief is contagious.

*David Grosch-Miller*

*Pray with the Wisconsin Conference of the United Church of Christ, twinned with the South Western Synod.*

**Read**   Isaiah 40:1-11; Mark 1:1-8

In the beginning
a voice cried out
over the desolation
across barren hills and into hopeless valleys,
*Make way! Make way!*

The voice took on the form of a man whose appearance startled.
The respectable murmured amongst themselves:
> *Can anything good come out of such a one?*
The sick and the suffering, though,
heard the voice and recognised the comfort in it.
It was like water flowing over stones, patient and sure,
or wind whistling through trees, timeless and untiring.
They flocked to the Jordan, eager to surrender burdens,
to be washed clean and made new.
They wanted to be free and open, ready for the coming of the Holy One.

Dear Lord,
give us ears to hear your song of salvation, whoever sings it.
Help us acknowledge our sickness, our suffering and our need for you.
Quench our thirst and smooth our rough places with your living water.
Blow through the deserts of our lives, levelling dunes of self-delusion
and filling in troughs of self-contempt.
Make our hearts free and open, ready to receive you.
Then give us a voice to cry out the good news all over our land:
*Here is our God, who chooses to dwell among us!  Make way!*

## The Lord loves justice *(Read Isaiah 61:8)*
(Human Rights Day – 10 December)

A separation barrier is being built between Israel and the Palestinian Territories. This barrier causes new headaches for farmers trying to reach their land and water sources. Major events, such as the olive harvest, and even routine tasks – weeding, fertilising and irrigating vegetables – can be stopped by closed gates or lack of a permit. Transport also becomes a problem, as farmers need permits to take vehicles and sometimes even donkeys, through the barrier gates.

> Kamil, 52, is a farmer in Kafr Sur in Tulkarem district. 'From January you need to fertilise olives, but I was not allowed to get to my olive grove for long enough. Olives need continuous care; neglect causes weeds to take hold. They get dry and settlers burn them and damage the trees. Last year, I could see the destruction but I couldn't reach the trees to save them'.

In the Gaza Strip, most Palestinian farmers are smallholders with an average of three to five dunums (12-20 acres) of land. 'They are among the poorest of Palestinians and becoming poorer,' says Ahmed Sourani of PARC (Palestinian Agricultural Relief Committees) in Gaza. Farmers producing greenhouse vegetables face serious problems in marketing their produce – currently they consume 40 to 60 per cent of their crop because there is no access to markets in the West Bank and beyond, and prices are very low. Some have contracts for strawberries or carnations with Agrexco, the Israeli marketing company, but it pays a lower price compared with prices paid to farmers in Israel. Furthermore, Palestinian farmers often have to compete with settlements in selling produce for export. The withdrawal of Israeli settlements from the Gaza Strip will not improve this situation as Israel will still control the borders.

*Christian Aid's report 'Facts on the Ground', October 2004*

*Pray for PARC, a Commitment for Life partner.*

It's alright for you, Lord God!
Your time is endless for making promises,
and you have all eternity to fulfil them!
But see how impatient we are –
see how we humans want everything now!

Is that why you make us wait
for the right time and place?
Are you teaching us patience still?

Lord God we confess
that we want things to happen yesterday.
We want peace and justice today
and not tomorrow.
We want equality and freedom in the present
and not as a promise for  the future.
We want to see your Kingdom come
in our time.
Waiting for your time
sometimes makes us doubt.

Lord, show us the breadth of your vision for the world.
Help us to grasp it, to hold it and keep it,
treasuring all that you promise;
keeping faith, staying hopeful
until your time comes.

## O Sad and Troubled Bethlehem

O sad and troubled Bethlehem,
we hear your longing cry
for peace and justice to be born
and cruel oppression die.
How deep your need for that great gift
of love in human form,
let Christ in you be seen again
and hearts by hope made warm.

While morning stars and evening stars
shine out in your dark sky,
despair now stalks your troubled streets
where innocents still die.
And Jesus, child of Mary,
whose love will never cease,
feels even now your pain and fear,
longs with you for your peace.

Amazingly and lovingly
Jesus, the child, has come
and brought to birth through human pain,
makes broken hearts his home.
He comes to comfort all who weep,
to challenge every wrong
and, living with the weak and poor,
becomes their hope, their song.

*Wendy Ross-Barker*

*Pray with the Nauru Congregational Church, one of the smallest of our
CWM partners (CWM Pacific Region).*

Compassionate, liberator God,
thank you for sharing your life in Christ with us,
to liberate us and save us from the time of trouble.

Liberate us from the bondage of sin that destroys your image in us.
Liberate us from the anger that harms our relationship with others.
Liberate us from envy that is the stumbling block to our growth in you.
Liberate us from our pride which stops us being a servant in your service.

Help us to remember the joy of liberation in your coming in Christ.
Help us to share our joy with others.
Help us to be sensitive to human needs.
Help us to give ourselves to the service of others.

Make our hearts to be a manger for Christ.
Mould our minds so we will act justly
and so fulfil the purpose of your birth.
Purify our hearts and fortify our determination
in order to serve you in this world.

## God with us

Mrs Soriana is thirty-five years old.  Six years ago she and her husband, with their five children, migrated from the country in a very poor area of Brazil to a shanty town on the outskirts of Salvador.  Lack of work had left them extremely poor, and they had no choice but to move.

The struggle to live continued.  Firstly, there was the difficulty of finding somewhere to live, and then followed the equally difficult search for work for Mr Soriana.  His wife was able to make a little money by opening a small shop in their house, where she sold a few items like soft drinks.

In due course she joined a small group of mothers who met once a week with a worker attached to the church in their district.  One evening a couple of weeks before Christmas, the group read St Luke's account of the birth of Jesus.  This is how she described her experience: 'Suddenly, while we were talking, we began to see how real this story was for us.  All of us know what hardship is and how difficult our lives are.  And here we heard about God's son being born, not in a big house, but in a poor place.
It was like one of our houses where there is no water or electricity.  It helped us to understand that God came among poor people and that he cares about us.  When someone cares about you, you begin to feel that you matter.  When you know that God cares about you, you begin to feel strong'.

> Blessed art thou, O Christmas Christ,
> that thy cradle was so low that shepherds,
> poorest and simplest of earthly folk,
> could yet kneel beside it,
> and look level-eyed into the face of God.
> *Anon.*

*Pray for all who this Christmas are in desperate need, who do not have enough food or water, or are without a place to call home.*

## Such a surprise!

**Read**   Luke 2:1-14

Lord Jesus,
it could have been so different!
You could have come
with lightning flash, drum rolls,
strobe lights and fanfares.
But you chose hay instead of down,
shepherds first, not kings,
angels' song instead of trumpets,
surprising us with your coming.

Great God,
thank you that you can still surprise
even the most cynical of us.
Thank you
that your humility shames our pride;
that your riches expose our greed;
that your love challenges our indifference.

God of surprises,
today we come to praise you,
seeing you in the faces of those we love,
and finding you still in the unexpected.

Thank you for the awe and wonder
that we can *still* feel
in a self centred and self satisfied world.
Thank you that you *still* come,
surprising earth with heaven,
transforming all creation
by your presence.

## The light is shining

CWM missionary nurse to Bangladesh Gillian Rose sent 48 patients from Bollobhpur Hospital for operations by a team from the Bangladesh National Hospital for the Blind which was visiting the region. She said: 'My own special patient was a tiny elderly beggar woman from a distant village who could see nothing at all. She had managed to beg and save up half the cost of the operation. Several others were unable to pay anything and had their expenses paid from our office'.

'With what joy they all emerged from the clinic four days later! I found my tiny beggar woman radiant with smiles. 'You are wearing a white coat and a green sari', she cried ecstatically. 'I can see everything. I can see!.'

The Bangladesh National Hospital for the Blind visits the region once a year. To discourage the sense of dependency on charity patients are asked to contribute towards the cost of treatment.

The Church of Bangladesh's Social Credit Development programme gives new hope to poor people. For example, a woman has been able to start a profitable business making toothpicks out of wire because of a loan from the scheme. Other projects supported by this programme include training in tie-dying, tailoring and crafts. It also helps run after-school clubs, which offer extra tuition for disadvantaged children from slum areas. In doing this, the church is not just looking after its own people, but is reaching out to Muslims in the slums, whose own community have forgotten them. The church is reaching out freely and with no strings attached.

*Pray with the Church of Bangladesh (CWM South Asia Region).*

**Read**    Isaiah 61:10-62:3; Psalm 148; Galatians 4:4-7;
            Luke 2:22-40

Light of the world,
having dawned upon your people,

we step into your light;
>       your light which is glory,
>       your light which is beauty,
>       your light which is the revelation of the truth –
>          that God is love,
>       that salvation is here.
>       The time of God's favour is **NOW.**

We step into your light;
>       your light which reveals our inner thoughts,
>       your light which causes us to fall in our shame,
>       your light which enables us to rise by your mercy.

We step into your light;
>       your light which clears away our wrong,
>       your light which declares us your daughters and sons,
>       your light which covers us in righteousness
>       and makes us a crown of beauty in your hand.

We, your children,
>       come to dedicate ourselves to you –
>       that we might honour the name you give us,
>       and reveal your light to others,
>       that all may become heirs to your kingdom.

## Christmas giving – an Indian perspective

Epiphany, which means 'appearing' or 'appearance' of God, is the climax of the Christmas season. One theme of Epiphany is the gifts brought by the magi. It is surprising that these gifts were brought by Gentiles rather than the Jews, which shows that the universal expectation of his Messianic arrival carries beyond Palestine. The gifts which the magi brought were valuable, and were suitable for offering to a king. But Matthew's purpose was not to focus on the magi's gifts. Rather, he wanted to inform through the incident that the magi, though Gentile foreigners, recognised Jesus as a king whose reign would one day accept them.

It is surprising to see how Christians the world over succumb to the commercial side of Christmas. Christmas is often celebrated by sharing gifts with one another. I remember our first Christmas in the UK; some of the church members gave gifts for my children, who were very happy and pleased about it. But they did not understand why they were given the presents. Immediately my younger son asked, 'is it for Christmas that we are receiving presents? If it is for Christmas then Jesus should receive the presents because it is his birthday that we are celebrating'.

In so many places Christmas ends up with commercial buying and exchange of gifts, whether we are Christians or not, and this gift-sharing becomes part of everyone's life. Rich people will say that they have money with which to buy gifts. But they don't realise that they are creating a tradition for the younger generation, and which can compel poor people to borrow money in order to buy gifts. Those who have can share: those do not have, have been forced to share. But giving does not need to be material sharing: being there for one another is a great gift. God's love revealed to us in Jesus is the greatest gift of all. This is the gift which should be shared with others.

*Jasmine Jebakani*

*Pray that all may come to know God's gift of Jesus.*

# Epiphany of the Lord

## Read  Matthew 2:1-12

As we celebrate the occasion of Epiphany,
remember God's revelation is Jesus Christ.
Remember God's gift to us in Jesus Christ.
Remember the people who have nothing to share materially.
Pray that they might realise and remember God's gift
for every one of us.
Pray for the people who feel lonely at this time of joyful occasion;
help them to realise that the Epiphany is the appearance of God,
which makes everyone a companion, taking away the lonely situation.

Give thanks to God for the gift God has given in Jesus Christ.
Thank God for sharing his life amidst the sufferings of this world.
Thank God for sharing his life with us in human flesh.

**God is good, he is with us, his grace is for all**
God is good for those who love their neighbours as themselves.
**God is good…**
God is good for those who are concerned for orphans and widows,
the destitute and all the underprivileged.
**God is good…**
God is good for those who work to bring peace among the nations.
**God is good…**
God is good for those who work to bring peace among religions.
**God is good…**
God is good for those who struggle to establish a just society.
**God is good…**
God is good for all those who share their talents and gifts for the welfare
of others.
**God is good…**

*If this prayer is used in public worship, the various petitions could be
illustrated by relevant pictures on power point or overhead projector,
and the words in heavy type used as a congregational response.*

## A pastor's story

Serving three congregations in one province of Zimbabwe, 60 to 90km apart, has been the most challenging time in my ministry. Usually I travel to each of my churches for pastoral reasons. This trip was so different. After travelling on a bus for 65 km, we then walked 15km on foot to get to where the church is. The roads were damaged during the rainy season 7 years ago and were never repaired. As we walked closer, everyone we met on the road had very pale and sad faces, because a drought had hit the area. For the past two years no rains had come, and all the reserves of food had long been finished. As we passed each village people followed us with the hope that we might have brought some food, but we only had our bibles, and money for the transport. A minister of the gospel walking on their roads raised all the hopes of the villagers, and yet I had nothing to offer.

Later I learnt that people were living on leaves and the roots of trees. I was horrified that I did not know what to do.

International donors were never allowed to visit an area such as this. Government aid was not used in this area because the people did not vote for the 'right' party. Yet the outside world was told that we have enough reserves. Looking at these people I doubted such publicity.

What is it that we can offer in such a world that we live in? More than ever in my 10 years of ministry I felt hopeless; yet my faith is a source of great strength and comfort to me; without it I'm sure I would be deeply unhappy. As I write some rains have come, and small-scale farming is happening again.

I now believe that suffering can be our greatest friend. It forces us to take a good look at our lives, to stand back and observe from a different perspective. If life were perfect here, there will be no desire to seek God.

*Revd Simbarashe Agushito*

*Pray with the Uniting Presbyterian Church in Southern Africa (CWM Africa Region).*

**Read**   Genesis 1:1-5 Psalm 29; Acts 19:1-7; Mark 1:4-11

God of time and tide,
we fear for our future, and our children's future;
for we are all in the same boat now, drifting in dangerous waters.
We are afraid of what happens when the ice caps melt,
or when the angry poor, with nothing to lose, rise up
and overwhelm a world we once thought safe.
We fear the last and dreadful baptism of your judgement.
We hear the Baptist's warning, mocking our complacency:
'Who told you to flee the wrath to come?'
We are afraid of the rising tide.

Yet amid the crashing waves your voice is heard:
"This is not the end," you say.
"This is still day one;
evening and morning of the first day."
For it is you, our Maker, who rules the rising tide.
It is your Son who comes up from the waters to promise a new day.
It is your Spirit, sweeping over the face of the waters,
who descends on him, and us.
A different baptism:
a baptism of liberation and love for all humanity.

Creator of the ocean depths,
Lord of the first day,
God of Christ our Saviour:
you know our fear and see us drown in guilt.
Lift us up, with your Son, out of the deep waters.
Baptise us with your Spirit,
and restore in us enough hope and courage
to face your new day with confidence,
for the sake of our children and all the world,
at the turning of the tide.

## Your servants are listening

In 1993 an English Bible camp was started by a local congregation of the Reformed Church in Budapest. Young Christians were invited from Oxford to teach a group of 45 Hungarian students, aged 13-23. Donations from Christians in the UK enabled students from neighbouring countries whose mother tongue is Hungarian to participate. So students from Hungary, Britain, Ukraine, Romania, Slovakia, Slovenia, and Croatia met in the name of Jesus.

The camp, which has continued ever since, is meant both for learning English and for spiritual development, with the focus on the Bible. Each morning there is a teaching session with songs – an excellent way to develop pronunciation and the rhythm of language, as well as learn new vocabulary. The Bible passage is introduced, and sketches used to explain unfamiliar words. Students then break into groups to discuss the passage and draw out its meaning linguistically and spiritually. Afternoon activities include sports, language-based games and quizzes, and drama. Various aspects of British culture are introduced and themes explored in a variety of ways.
The evening talks aim at leading young people to faith and commitment. Topics include God's grace through Jesus, the need to persevere, God's discipline for the believer, and true faith. Talks are translated into Hungarian by some of the more able students. On Sunday the campers go to the local church where they perform songs they have learnt.

'The true sign of being a Christian is how we live our lives', says one of the campers. 'This is the most powerful testimony to God's love'.

It is hoped that the spiritual formation taking place here will continue to spread, and shape the growth of God's church in Hungary.

*Erzsebet Ábráham*

*Pray for the Reformed Church in Hungary.*

**Read** 1 Samuel 3:1-10 (11-20); Psalm 139:1-6, 13-18;
John 1:43-51

Encompassing God, behind me and before,
still me in the darkness of winter nights,
to hear your unique word;
shape me in the grey of winter's noon to know your call.
Prepare me to expect your action –
**do something, O God . . . to make my ears tingle,
for here I am.**

Renewing One, help us hear your voice;
then clear our eyes to see your way,
enable our ears to hear the needs of others,
expose in us all we hide, even from ourselves –
**do something, O God . . . to make our ears tingle,
for here we are.**

Calling Jesus, go on calling,
give us hearts and minds to be honest disciples;
move us from cynicism and doubt to utter trust and faith.
Never let us fool ourselves in the way we live out your call,
transform us, with integrity of body, mind and spirit;
**find us, O God . . . in every conversation,
every commitment, every relationship.**

Creative Spirit, uniquely equipping, inspiring our response;
call us with your words of life, bear us up upon your wings,
turn faith into action to work for change,
to bring fullness of life to all who yearn for it.
**Work in us something, O God . . .
to make all ears tingle with your Living Word,
for we are yours.**

## A divided church seeks unity in a divided land

Christianity came to Korea first through the influence of the Jesuits in
1784.  The Protestants arrived one hundred years later, in the shape
of a Korean man, who built the first Protestant church in Hwanghae
Province in the north, and an American medical missionary, a female
doctor who founded the Jesus hospital in Jeon Ju, in the south.
One of the first acts of the early Protestants, assisted by Revd John Ross,
a Scottish Presbyterian minister serving in Manchuria, was to translate
the entire new testament into Hangul, the common language of the
people.  In 1907, the Presbyterian Church of Korea was established,
and the first Korean pastors ordained.  From the beginning, Korean
Christians and their partner British, American and Canadian
missionaries built schools, orphanages, hospitals, clinics and churches,
many of which still stand today.  Today 25% of South Korea is Christian.
Eighteen percent of those are Presbyterians, numbering 7 million in
about 30,000 churches.

The Presbyterian church in South Korea, however, is divided.  Currently
there are more than 130 Presbyterian denominations.  Over the decades,
they have divided over Biblical interpretation and methods of study,
the articulation of Christian theology from a Korean perspective, and
political activity.  Now two of the largest Presbyterian denominations
– the Presbyterian Church of Korea (PCK) and the Presbyterian Church
in the Republic of Korea (PROK) – have sought out the United Reformed
Church to learn about ecumenism and unity.  Despite their differences,
which are significant and which persist, they now seek a way to live
together in peace and unity, to be a sign and a symbol of God's reign
and the peoples' hopes for national reunification.

The pain of a Korea divided between North and South is great among
the people in the south.  Pray for the efforts of the Presbyterian church
to overcome division and find unity, as they work with the people for
peace and unity on the peninsula.

*Carla Grosch-Miller*

*Pray for Christian unity in every country, especially your own.*

**Read**  Mark 1:14-20

Fresh from forty days of fasting,
thin but determined,
the Word walked along the seashore.

The sun bounced off waves,
flashed in nets thrown high then sunk low,
glistened the sweat on backs of men hard at work.

The Word spoke: *Follow.*
The men dropped their nets and followed.
No greater test of faith necessary.
No assent to doctrine or ecclesiology.

Lord, at the moment of decision,
enable us to grasp the essential:
your call and claim on our lives.
Help us to leave behind that which stands
in the way of our *yes,*
that we may work hand in hand
with our brothers and sisters
whom you also called,
as, together, we fish for people.

## Leprosy Mission Sunday

Sarah Amongin is now a healthy, happy woman; but it wasn't always like that.  As a young wife Sarah lived, as was expected, with her husband and his family.  Her mother-in-law noticed patches on Sarah's skin which are the first signs of leprosy.  She took Sarah to Kumi hospital, in a district of Uganda, where the disease was confirmed.

However, her mother-in-law still thought of leprosy like everyone else: that the victim is being punished by God for their sins, or being cursed by evil spirits.  Also, a sick person is a great financial burden.  Consequently, Sarah's husband abandoned her and their children, and her mother-in-law forced them to leave.

By now, Sarah had lost part of a finger because she had scalded herself whilst cooking one day, and, because leprosy causes people to loose their ability to feel, had not noticed.  The burn was so bad that she had to have the finger amputated.  Fortunately, she had a friend who let her stay for a while, and through Kumi hospital she was cured of leprosy with no further disabilities.

She was now a single mother with no way of earning a living.  Kumi hospital came to the rescue, with a practical way of getting out of poverty.  They provided a loan of around £100, with which she bought an ox and plough.  She began farming, and despite the incredibly hard work involved, she became independent and able to feed her children.  With this independence the power of poverty and stigma was broken.  Her husband recognised that she was cured and a respectable woman, and returned to her.  He now has an ox, so they farm together.

The Leprosy Mission works hard to provide a holistic approach that enables each person to be completely restored: physically, emotionally, socially, and by God's grace, spiritually.  Socio-economic rehabilitation projects offer education, vocational training, small-business loans, and sanitation/housing improvement.

*Pray for the work of The Leprosy Mission all over the world.*

**Read**    Deuteronomy 18:15-20; Psalm 111; 1 Corinthians 8:1-13

O Lord our God, you came into this world
as a threat to all that was unclean.
Our human senses fail to spot all that stands in between
your Word and our world; some bits seen and most not seen.

Hence we pray, you within us, send us Moses, send us Paul,
to challenge us, to nurture us, to lead and guide and tell us all
to heed the prophet within us, around us, surround us,
because our understanding of you is too small.

Small minds, small hearts, confused perceptions, blinkered views;
great are you, praise the Lord; we have you.
Let your mighty hand drag all unclean attributes
from our hearts, so Moses, Paul and you may grow within us.

May we remember lepers who are called 'unclean'.
Ease their suffering, ease their pain, thank you for our 'skin clean'.
But heal our diseased spirit; send to us then, as to Moses and Paul,
the health and wealth of your Word this world to redeem.

## Faith in action

There are different ways of describing a church. We could talk about statistics. The United Church of Zambia (UCZ) has around 2.5million members. It is the largest Protestant church in Zambia, and is divided into Presbyteries like Lusaka which is linked with the Wessex Synod. Lusaka is typically divided into ten consistories and has a bishop, elected for four years.

Or we could talk about vision – in this case, a vision of unity and mission. When Zambia came into being in 1964, what was to prevent the churches from uniting? The churches founded by the Church of Scotland, the Paris Missionary Society and the Methodist Church came together, and today they sustain a dynamic programme of evangelism and social services.

Revd Norman Francis, a Jamaican minister, who is in Zambia participating in the CWM Clergy Xchange programme, describes being involved in a gruelling pastoral schedule – walking for 5 hours, then praying with people in quick succession. On one Sunday he baptised 95 babies and children, and was told of a local minister who had once baptised 300 children in a morning service.

But the country, and the church, also faces huge social and economic challenges. Total debt cancellation would seem to be the only solution to many of these, but although the government has fulfilled the prescriptions of the World Bank and the IMF to the letter, they feel that they cannot at present achieve the HIPIC benchmarks without increasing poverty to unacceptable levels. Thanks to combined Church-government initiatives, HIV/AIDS prevalence has gone down from 20% to 15%. There are huge numbers of AIDS orphans and traditional systems of care are stretched to the limit as families adopt the children of relatives as their own. With slender financial resources, the UCZ runs health centres and secondary schools and projects such as HODEP, which currently enables fifty-five orphans to receive full-time education. This is a peaceful and friendly country, with strong cultural values; and the Church is widely respected and trusted.

*Pray with the United Church of Zambia (CWM Africa Region), twinned with the Wessex Synod.*

**Read**  Isaiah 40:21-31; Mark 1:29-39

Brother Jesus,
we remember your strong hands
on the fevered forehead of Simon Peter's mother-in-law;
your gentle insistence that she stand,
as you willed her back to health;
her deep gratitude and eager service in response.
How quickly good news spreads!
In a matter of hours,
the whole city was at your door, with ills of every kind,
begging a touch from those strong and gentle hands.

We, too, need your touch;
for we are weak and tired and sick.
Our fevered pursuit of worldly goods and earthly security
has left us weary and empty.
Our diet of rich foods, while others beg for crumbs,
has made us sick in body and in soul.

Lift us up.
Gently insist that we stand.
Will us back to health.
Beckon us to follow you into the deserted place,
and teach us to pray,
so that our strength may be renewed
and we may mount up with wings like eagles.

Then we shall run and not be weary, walk and not faint,
as we spend our lives in deep gratitude and eager service,
proclaiming the good news of your healing love.

## God, in your grace, transform the world

These words above are the theme of the 9th Assembly of the World Council of Churches, which meets from 14th-23rd February at Porto Alegre in Brazil.

The logo, on the page opposite, represents both the hand of God holding the creation and a praying human hand, incorporates the dove of peace and the covenant rainbow.  The shape and movement suggest a renewed and transformed world.  The colours used are red, like the WCC logo and the national colours of Brazil, yellow and blue. (see www.wcc-assembly.info for full colour copy)
The Assembly, which meets every 7 years, will be a time of encounter, prayer, celebration and reflection for thousands of Christians from around the world – over 700 delegates and their advisors representing over 340 member churches.

A highlight of the 9th Assembly will be the 'Mutirão' – a Portuguese word meaning:  coming together, celebrating together, reflecting together.

Three of the plenary sessions, each of which is to be viewed in the light of the overall theme, are:
- The unity of the church – this will reflect the conviction that divisive moral and ethical challenges should not cause Christians to lose sight of what is most fundamental to them all: the starting and ending point is the grace of God in Jesus Christ and the Spirit as mediated in the church and in creation.
- Overcoming poverty and economic injustice – the ecumenical movement is under obligation to judge the economic process at work in the world today in the light of the Gospel message.
- Decade to overcome violence: churches seeking reconciliation and peace (2001-2010) – Jesus reconciled us to God and with each other, proclaiming peace and a new relationship between those who had been separated by alienation and hostility.  Our endurance comes from the unceasing breath of the Holy Spirit in our hearts and in the life of the church.

*Pray for the work of the WCC Assembly.*

## Read    2 Kings 5:1-14; Mark 1:40-45

Healing Lord,
at one time or another
I have felt ugly, scarred and unlovable.
Illness and sorrows,
depression and darkness
are part of my human life.
Yet you touch me
as though I was already whole.
You take my ugliness,
my scars and ill health,
my depression and dark times,
and, as part of your loving,
you absorb them, and me,
into yourself.

Lord, when I feel
that the world is against me;
when my body is frail
and my mind is weak;
when tears are close
and heaven seems far away,
touch my soul,
touch my heart,
and say to me,
'Go, be whole.
All is well'.

Lord, heal my hurts;
hold me in your hand
until the night and the pain is past
and morning comes.

God, in your grace,
transform the world

**World Council of Churches**
**9th Assembly**
*14-23 February 2006*
*Porto Alegre, Brazil*

## No boundaries to compassion

The primary purpose of the fellowship of churches in the World Council of Churches is to call one another to visible unity ... expressed ... through witness and service to the world.

The function of the person giving diakonia (service) has been described as:
The go-between
* promotes mutuality – in that those who serve the needy accept their own need to give
* adds to the power of the needy to control what happens to them
* remains faithful and does not desert the needy, even when there are difficulties
* gives an account of him/herself to those served.

The agent
* shares the resources that promote life
* respects the judgement of the one in need as to what their needs are and how best they are met
* responds to immediate needs whilst understanding, resisting and transforming the systems which create and aggravate them.

The attendant or servant
* acts with those he/she claims to serve, and not for them or about them or over them
* puts the least advantaged first
* acknowledges the inevitable cost as well as the gain
* sets no boundary to its compassion.

*Pray for the work of the church world-wide as it seeks to respond to human need.*

**Read** Mark 2:1-13

We pray for the people who are ill.
Let the healing of God touch them to guide and uphold them.

We pray for all who are affected by HIV/AIDS.
Let the power of God give them strength to comfort and sustain them.

We pray for all who are affected by war and conflict.
Let the protector God protect them from danger.

We pray for all who are affected by natural disasters.
Let the creator God be present among them.

We pray for all who are disturbed in their mind.
Let the wisdom of God give them the knowledge of his peace.

We pray for all who are involved in helping people in healing.
Give them the strength of God to empower them.

God, the compassionate healer,
help us to show your compassion to all the victims of diseases and disasters.
Help us to be involved in the healing ministry along with others.
May our commitment be strong and steady as we serve.
May our choices be sensible and stable for the generation to come.

## Transfiguration in the valley

The S-Corner Organisation is located in one of the inner-city areas in Kingston, Jamaica, where lack of education and training, and teenage pregnancies, keep the residents in a cycle of poverty. S-Corner has been working hard for the past thirteen years to help the people there improve their lives, with programmes that target youths between the ages of 16-25, as well as the elderly who benefit particularly from a nutrition clinic.

Kevin is a 25-year old who lives with his parents and four siblings in a two-bedroom house, sharing the bathroom/toilet with four other families in a tenement yard. His story is as follows:

"My mother wanted all her children to be 'somebody', especially her sons. She worked hard and sends me to school, sometimes without lunch money. But I didn't pass the subjects to get a good job, and college was out of the question without money; so me and my brothers start to hang out with the rest of the boys on the street. Some were real hard-core pickpockets but most of us just didn't know what to do with ourselves. Police see us; they don't like us so they beat us and take us to jail.

Then I heard that S-Corner placed students in skills programmes, but students first go through a literacy programme, which costs money. I asked the organiser if she could find a way to help me pay this fee so I could better myself.

Imagine my joy when two weeks later she said I could register for the programme because she had found someone to pay my fee plus the lunch money, to ensure I could complete the course, which I did. Now I am working in a community-based initiative – a block-making business, where I maintain a proper inventory and do the book keeping. I am now qualified to find a good job. I no longer sit on the street corner, my life has really changed, and I have hope for the future".

*Pray for the S-Corner Organisation in Jamaica, one of our Commitment for Life partners.*

Living God,
you who have chosen to reveal yourself
through all generations,
you come, and are not silent.

Among prophets, kings, and lowly people,
you have moved, spoken,
and revealed your face.
You have revealed
a might and power based on love and sacrifice,
not on fear,
a judgement and a covenant demand
based on mercy and compassion, not condemnation,
a presence and a purpose based on peace and healing,
and not destruction.

This is your light and glory,
the holy beauty which emanates,
which radiates, which declares your presence,
which penetrates skin and bone
to the heart of our being,
where we are touched by heaven's smile -
cleansed and healed,
our selves beautified,
our selves revealed as you see us;
delightfully filled with all the potential of your image alive in us.

We can say no more,
can do no more,
but welcome your light,
rest in your glory,
and worship you.

Joel 2:1-2, 12-17 or Isaiah 58:1-12
Psalm 51:1-17
2 Corinthians 5:20b-6:10
Matthew 6:1-6, 16-21

## Have mercy, O God

A bishop in the Church of South India has launched a scathing attack on the church's hypocrisy towards lower castes.
"In the Indian church, the caste system comes before Christ", said Bishop Devasahayam of Chennai Diocese, himself a Dalit. "Caste blood is thicker than Christ's blood that we share. Caste is seen as the primary identity even in the church. If caste is true, Christianity cannot be true". He criticised the church for such practices as keeping separate cemeteries for Dalits and non-Dalits, and said that the church was biased towards upper castes in its development policies, because it had sold off church properties in rural areas to build large churches in urban areas. Also the church's set readings and prayers do not include prayers to bless the huts of the Dalits.

Bishop Devasahayam called for action, 'Can we make a declaration that we will not entertain caste practices and prejudices in the church?'.

Meanwhile, in South Africa, research by the South African Council of Churches has found that racial segregation and unfair treatment of black ministers is still rife in the churches there. Black ministers are often paid less and placed in ill-equipped rural churches. This has the potential to split the churches along racial lines, and prominent church leaders have called on the churches to start confronting racism head on.

Think of anything in the life of YOUR church, at local or national level, of which we should repent.

Leader: On this day we recognise our sin;
**ALL:** **Each one of us unholy,**
**living in an unholy world.**
Leader: And on this day when we recognise our sin,
we recognise the one made sin who knew no sin,
so that in him we might become
the righteousness of God.
**ALL:** **Jesus, you bring light to our darkness,**
**proclaiming the day of salvation,**
**the negation of our sin in the sight of God.**
Leader: On this day we recognise our sin
and come before God in brokenness and contrition;
we recognise that this momentary attitude of heart
is not enough.
**ALL:** **Let us not hide the light of forgiveness**
**and freedom which you have given;**
**but let us reveal your light in concrete terms –**
**undoing injustice, releasing the captive,**
**sharing our bread with the hungry.**
Leader: As on this day we recognise our sin
we pray not only for forgiveness
and the assurance of pardon,
but a spirit willing to play her part
in revealing the light of Christ given for the world.
**ALL:** **God of Grace, of truth, of mercy,**
**restore to us the joy of your salvation,**
**and sustain in us a willing spirit -**
**to demonstrate your righteous heart,**
**attending to our neighbours far and near,**
**with faith and action hand in hand,**
**not seeking our reward,**
**but the honour of your name.**

## Fairtrade Fortnight

The FAIRTRADE mark is an independent consumer label which appears on products as a guarantee that:
- Farmers receive a fair and stable price for their products
- Farmers and plantation workers have extra income and the opportunity to improve their lives
- There is a greater respect for the environment
- Small-scale farmers gain a stronger position in world markets
- There is a closer link between consumers and producers.

More than 5 million people – farmers, workers and their families – across 49 developing countries, benefit from the international Fairtrade system.

A 2004 MORI poll showed that the number of people who recognised the FAIRTRADE mark had doubled to 39% since 2002. Fairtrade sales are currently doubling every two years, and all the major supermarket chains now stock Fairtrade products. More than 700 products carrying the FAIRTRADE mark are now available across the retail catering sectors. It is thought that retail sales in 2004 will top £130 million. Fairtrade brands now account for 18.8% of the total UK roast and ground coffee market. Cafédirect owns the sixth largest coffee brand, and it has developed Teadirect into one of the fastest growing tea brands in the UK.

Fairtrade Fortnight is promoted by networks around the country including CAFOD, Christian Aid, Oxfam, Tearfund, SCIAF, Traidcraft Exchange, and the World Development Movement.
(see: www.fairtrade.org.uk).

*Pray for the increasing use of fairly traded goods through out the world.*

**Read** Genesis 9:8-17; Psalm 25:1-10; 1 Peter 3:18-22;
Mark 1:9-15

Your journey did not begin, Lord Jesus,
on a yellow brick road with loyal friends
and an easy rainbow promise.
You started out alone, in a wilderness of hunger and doubt,
tempted by shortcuts, wondering which way to go.
And the Spirit that blessed your baptism drove you there,
testing any notion you may have had
that being beloved of God would assure you of special protection.

Yet it was in finding your way through the wilderness
that you learnt how to walk the terrible road to Jerusalem.
It was in facing your aloneness that you learnt to keep company
with those who would make easy promises before letting you down.
It was in wrestling with your demons that you learnt to take on death
– a death that would kill the body and free the soul.
It was in your hunger and weakness that you touched imprisoned souls
for whom saving arks and rainbow covenants had no meaning.

Enter again, Lord Jesus, the wilderness of our world:
the places of hunger and doubt and imprisoned souls,
where people are locked in their cells or themselves,
and whole nations are trapped in war, oppression, debt.

And enter my own wilderness, when I cannot find my bearings.
Search out the lost child in me, the wild beasts and angels in me,
the parts of me that are still imprisoned in the sins of my youth,
the unresolved fragments and loose ends of my life.

Walk with me, with us, Lord Jesus,
through the wildernesses of our time,
so that we may walk with you this Lent,
towards your cross and ours.

## The poor shall eat

Kapasule is the first village in the Chikwawa district of Malawi to benefit from the Fairtrade premium received by the local Cane Growers' Association. Now local people have their own supply of clean, fresh water. Before the borehole was dug, women and children had to carry water in containers for 1.5 km from a nearby village. It is the first of many improvements planned for local villages, paid for with the premium. The village chief explains, "There are more than 500 people in the village, and only some of them are farming cane sugar; but all are benefiting from the water. We have plans for the future. We want to improve the local hospital and also build a community day secondary school, so that village children can get there easily. We would like people in the UK to buy more sugar than at present, since the more premium we can get, the more we can help our community'.

Estellia Ditala is a widow. Eight people live with her in a brick house with broken mud floors. There is a table, but no chairs, and two pottery jugs for water. Estellia is the only breadwinner. She says things have been difficult, but money earned through sugar means her family can eat meat twice a week. She only ever has a day off when she is sick. Like the other farmers she starts work at 4.00 am, when it is cooler. By midday it is so hot that everyone is drenched with sweat. Estellia says that the best moment was seeing all the children who would normally have to walk 1.5 km to fetch water, laughing as they filled their containers at the village bore hole.

*Pray with the Church of Christ in Malawi (CWM Africa Region).*

# With you all things are possible

**Read** Genesis 17:1-7, 15-16; Psalm 22:23-31; Romans 4:13-25; Mark 8:31-38

Creating God, in whose time the generations come and go,
you promise life here and now and into eternity.
**With you all things are possible,**
    the poor shall eat and be hungry no more.
Life will continue, even unborn children will praise you,
growing in your likeness in faithful love and commitment.

Self-giving Jesus, you show us your way of loyal service
that loves beyond the limits, and brings new life.
**With you all things are possible,**
    prisoners are promised freedom, the frightened find release.
May we reveal your kindness in words and deeds
that honour you and multiply all praises.

Life-giving Spirit, you show us God whom we know in Jesus,
help us stand firm in faith and witness to your goodness.
**With you all things are possible,**
    for you call into existence the things that do not exist
and enable us to hope in the face of all impossibility.
Strengthen our commitment to follow and never to turn away.

All-embracing God of Love,
in this world of wonder and of suffering we promise to praise you.
**With you all things are possible,**
    we will risk our lives for you and live your kingdom life,
we will resist fear and speak plainly of your way and truth,
your angels will rejoice and not feel ashamed as we walk with you.

## Loving and being loved

The Gospel tells us that the first commandment is to love God with everything we've got – heart and soul and mind and strength; and that the second is to love our neighbour as ourselves. But love cannot simply be commanded.

The phrase 'the love of God' can become too familiar, too routine, something we believe in as a part of our faith, and take for granted. The God of the Bible is not a cold and unfeeling God, but warm and even passionate. God's love is not something abstract, an aspect of the official policy for humankind. God doesn't just love us in a general way along with everyone else. God is '*my* god', as the psalmists say, who loves each of us in a deeply personal way, as someone who is unique and precious, to whom he has given life. God doesn't just love in a formal way: but wants us for himself. God has a heartfelt desire for us to be with him, as a mother relates to her little child.

One of the basic elements of silent prayer is simply letting ourselves be loved. Perhaps this is part of the meaning of Jesus' saying that we need to become like little children. In the stillness we can remind ourselves that God loves us unconditionally, now, just as we are. We can let ourselves be enfolded and wrapped in the love of God, letting God put his/her arms around us to hold us.

To let ourselves be loved in this way is not self-indulgent or narrowly self-centred: it is the seed or source of our love for God and other people. For as we sense that God loves and wants us, just the way that we are, we find ourselves warming towards God ... and it is from this that our love of neighbour grows.

*Sandy Ryrie – from an occasional paper maintaining a link*
*with those interested in silent or contemplative prayer*

*Pray with the United Church in the Solomon Islands*
*(CWM Pacific Region).*

**Read** Exodus 20:1-17; John 2:13-22

I am a woman with an unclean heart,
No light dusting will do; I need a good scrub.

For I have made of my own desires a god.
It is my comfort and my convenience that matter most to me.

I have fashioned idols of bank balances and stock portfolios;
In sterling I trust.

I have cursed drivers hogging the second lane,
and called George W Bush the anti-Christ behind his back.

I have made Sunday my shopping, read the paper, laze around day.

I have blamed my parents for my failures,
and attributed my meagre successes to my own elbow grease.

I have the blood of the innocent on my hands;
I have been silent in the face of the killing fields of war and hatred.

I have lusted in my heart….and other places, too.

I have stolen pens, pads of paper and paper clips from workplaces.

I love gossip.

I want a good singing voice, thick curly hair and more shoes
than any one person should have.  I also wouldn't mind a new car.

Yet, Lord, you love me still.  I don't know why.
Hose me down, scour the baked-on bits, and rinse me clean.
Then I'll be as good as new.  Thank you.

## From darkness to light

Papua New Guinea's capital Port Moresby is the worst of the 130 world capitals surveyed by the Economist Intelligence Unit. It consistently scores highest in the unit's 'hardship' table due to its poverty, crime, poor health care and a rampant gang culture. Port Moresby has a population of just 250,000, but a survey of international crime shows that the murder rate is 23 times that of London. This is blamed on 'raskol' gangs, said to have carried out violence ranging from bank robberies with machine guns to car hold-ups with machetes. Raskols say they are provoked into such acts by police who use violence on them when they are in custody. They also argue that their crimes are driven by poverty. Basic food items such as rice are beyond the means of many families. Unemployment is estimated to be between 60 and 90 per cent.

Papua New Guinea faces other challenges, such as the spread of HIV/AIDS, sexual and domestic violence, and marriage breakdown.
The Moderator of the United Church in Papua New Guinea, Revd Samson Lowa says, 'The problems of our country can seem so overwhelming that they can almost cripple us. We have adopted the approach of starting by making an impact in a small way. Our focus is the family. To deal with the social issues we need to invest the gospel in family, children and youth.
Samson Lowa preaches on a 20 minute radio show called 'Strentin family na strongin Papua New Guinea' – straighten out family, strengthen Papua New Guinea. The church also organises street meetings for people to discuss and share ideas on how to deal with their problems. Its Women's Fellowship has organised itself to address in particular domestic violence and HIV/AIDS.

*Pray with the United Church in Papua New Guinea*
*(CWM Pacific Region).*

**Read** Numbers 21:4-9; Psalm 107:1-3, 17-22;
Ephesians 2:1-10; John 3:14-21

Creator God, the Mother God,
we thank you for who we are, for we are what you have made us.
But we are sorry for what we have become;
for we are not what you have made us to be.
Dead we are already even though living this life.

It is the death we earn from sins.
So as we pray and sing the hymns
deliver us from the womb of death
into life's bounty breadth.

Gather us all from north and south,
filled with praises in our mouth.
Gather us all from east and west,
so we may become your chosen best.

Like those (Israelites) in wilderness,
who gave up faith while in distress;
we do the same being weak in faith,
you please accept our humanness.

Thank you, God, for our mothers
who nurtured us into this world.
We seek you, God, as our mother
to nurture us into your 'word'.

Lead us from Death to Life –
being from West this we pray.
Mrityorma Amritamgamya –
being from East this we say.

[1]*Sanskrit language words meaning From Death to Life
(pronounce as written, but with stress on 'g' in second word)*

## Following Jesus

Dear God,
use me to advertise your faithful love.
Send me to proclaim your love and forgiveness.

And when I complain that I am not clever enough,
or old enough, or good enough,
remind me how you have taken ordinary people
and given them your words to speak and your dreams to dream.

Give me confidence to use what gifts and talents I have,
 so that you are seen to be the power behind me
and the vision ahead of me.

Give me speech, which is sensitive and strong,
increasing compassion and destroying ignorance
by what I say and how I say it.

Give me insight which cuts deep and true,
uncovering what is evil and encouraging what is good.

Give me your spirit, promised by Jesus,
so I can discern the truth for my time
and be strengthened for my task.

And if you call me to new challenges which test my confidence
and stretch my vision of your love,
keep before me the sight of Jesus
battling with the tempter,
striding to Jerusalem,
facing the unknown.

*Pray with Gereja Presbyterian Malaysia (CWM East Asia Region).*

**Read**  Jeremiah 31:31-34; John 12:20–33

Lord of all,
we walk the wilderness way these 40 days,
through brambles and over rocks,
examining the desert of our desolation,
considering the distance between I and Thou.

You tell us to hate our lives and to embrace death.
We contemplate the consequences and count the cost.
We want to bear fruit, to be a sign of your abundance,
but we don't know if we have the courage to follow you.

Still our restless hearts compel us towards you.
Tune our ears to the thunder that will comfort and strengthen us.
Write your law on our hearts so that we can know no other.
Urge us forward on our lenten journey.
Prepare us for the many little deaths
that will bring us the life you have for us.
Make us wholly your own.

Bring us to the time
when death itself will be vanquished
and fear transfigured into hope
and your glory will shine forth
with a radiance unknown to human eyes.

And we will know you
as close as our breath.

**9 April**

Liturgy of the Palms:
Mark 11:1-11 or John 12:12-16  Psalm 118:1-2, 19-29
Liturgy of the Passion:
Isaiah 50:4-9a  Psalm 31:9-16  Philippians 2:5-11
Mark 14:1-15:47 or Mark 15:1-39 (40-47)

## Palm Sunday, 2005

'Inch by inch, the so-called Israeli security wall is blocking the main street that leads into the heart of Bethlehem. As I look at the surrounding hilltops, there I find it, standing 8 metres tall, gazing at me. Bethlehem, the cradle of Christianity, has become a big, crowded prison.

A wall? Is this the solution to the Palestinian-Israeli conflict? Every morning, tears come to my eyes as I observe the shade that the wall imposes on the green hills of Bethlehem. I feel powerless and helpless. Who can I object to? Is this peace and justice?

As I drive deeper into Bethlehem, I find myself in a society striving to survive in a city sealed off from the rest of the world. This will be one of the main cities of the future Palestinian state, surrounded by a cement wall that will limit its people's movement, its economic trade and its connection with the outside world. Slowly, the hunger to establish a viable Palestinian state and the fight to lift the Palestinian economy is dying as Palestinians witness the wall encircling Bethlehem. They slowly acknowledge that they are on their own in the fight for survival and that the strong overtake the weak in a world full of hatred and injustice. The dreams of statehood and freedom are intertwined with individual worries, such as putting bread on the table every night for children to eat. I ask myself again: 'Do my people, so eager to live free and independent, deserve this?'. *Zack Bernard Sabella*

On Palm Sunday, 2005, the local community of the Bethlehem area, joined by international visitors, sought to march from Bethlehem to Jerusalem. Since 1990, Palestinian Christians and Muslims are prohibited from entering Jerusalem, which deprives them of the basic right to worship in the Holy City. Therefore, the procession was intercepted by the Israeli army, at the military checkpoint between Bethlehem and Jerusalem.

Marchers walked with donkeys and carried palm branches, re-enacting the entry of Jesus to Jerusalem 2000 years ago: they also carried signs calling for freedom of worship, free access to Jerusalem, and the cessation of land confiscation and wall constructions.

*Pray for the peace of Jerusalem, and for a just and peaceful resolution to the Israeli-Palestinian conflict.*

## Palm Sunday and Passion Sunday

**Read** Mark 11:1-11; Psalm 118:1-2, 9-29

This is the day!  The day of your making!
A day to rejoice and be glad.
We will unlock the gates of our churches and towns,
we will open the doors of our hearts and our minds,
and invite you in, welcome you in.
Blessed, the one who comes!

And those who have followed will lead you now.
And those who have waited will carpet the ground.
And the blind will open their eyes to you.
And the stones will echo the hullabaloo,
and honour the chief corner stone.
And the festal procession will thread its way
through crowded streets and market place,
and into the house of the prayers of the nations.
This day is a day for all.

"Don't worry about tomorrow," you said.
And indeed there may be trouble ahead:
the tree to be cursed, the tables to turn,
the rage unforeseen, the pain unimagined,
and tears that none of us saw.
We'll take back the terrified colt in the morning
and face the music with you.
But today is the day to wave palms in the air,
and to shout our hosannas and dance.

But save us, good Lord, from instant romance.
Show us a faith that has further to go,
and gates that stay open, and praises that last,
and hope that endures when the crowds have gone home;
at the end of the day, show us love.

## All shall be well

*During Holy Week we shall be using the four stanzas of Gillian Heald's
meditation based on the best known saying of the medieval English mystic,
Julian of Norwich.*

In the pain of divorce and separation,
　　in the desolation of grief,
when it seems we are alone,
　　though many surround us;
as relationships break down,
　　fall apart and shatter,
cracked by loss of trust,
　　commitment and love;
in all this the crucified resurrected One is there –
　　at one –
at one with God,
　　with himself
　　　　and with all humanity,
bringing harmony in discord,
　　wholeness in brokenness –

For all shall be well
　　and all shall be well
　　　　and all manner of things shall be well.

*Pray with the Presbyterian Church of India
(CWM South Asia Region).*

**Read**   Isaiah 42:1-9; Hebrews 9:11-15

Lord of creation,
servant of your people,
what a wonderful, overwhelming love
you have for all of us!
In obedience to God's will
you chose the path to death,
and so fulfilled the prophecies of long ago;
by your sacrifice you have set us free.

But we don't act like people who are free –
free to live, to love, to serve!
Lord Jesus, too often the way we behave
denies your gift.
We act as slaves, of human desire,
to the restrictions of society,
and to the excesses of injustice and intolerance.
We are blinded by our self-interest,
crippled by traditions and history.

Set us free once more, Lord.
Open our eyes, unstop our ears,
unlock our lips, so that the sacrifice
of your life liberates us again.

For your silence was more eloquent than our clamour;
your determination was steady, unlike our wavering;
your justice and truth could be our crown and glory,
and through your sacrifice we are freed
only so that we can be your lamp for all nations.

## 11 April

Isaiah 49:1-7
Psalm 71:1-14
1 Corinthians 1:18-31
John 12:20-36

## And all shall be well

In the division between rich and poor,
        in the segregation of the haves and have nots,
when some live in magnificent mansions
        and others on squalid streets;
as the wealthy West draws back
        from engagement with injustice,
shutting out suffering humanity,
        all made in the image of God.
In all this the crucified resurrected One is there –
        at one –
at one with God,
        with himself
                and with all humanity,
bringing solidarity in suffering,
        wholeness in brokenness –

For all shall be well
        and all shall be well
                and all manner of things shall be well.

*Pray with the United Congregational*
*Church of Southern Africa*
*(CWM Africa Region).*

## Read   Hebrews 13:12-14

Outside – those who are considered outcastes, despised, marginalised?
Inside – those who are privileged to enjoy their life
without any hardship?
Jesus also suffered with those who are outside the gate.
Going with him to the outside will include those who are inside.
Christ's suffering gathers and unites everyone,
Jews and Gentiles together in God's love.

God's love is revealed in the birth
as well as in the death of Jesus Christ.
Christ's death on the cross is the extreme symbol
of his love for humanity.
The Cross is the symbol of forgiveness as well as suffering.

God of Love,
give us wisdom to understand the pain and suffering
you have experienced.
Help us to demonstrate solidarity with all who suffer.
Help us to take the cross of humbleness so that we respect each other.
Help us to take the cross of compassion so that we love each other.
Help us to take the cross of obedience to follow your footsteps.
Help us to take the cross of courage
to suffer with those who are outside the city gate.
Help us to take the cross of strength
to work for unity amongst diversity.

Loving God,
the ways of your son Jesus Christ are our path;
the words of Jesus Christ are our shield.
His death on the cross gave us life.
May you, who led us in the past, continue to lead us in the future.

## And all manner of things shall be well

In the confusion of mental illness,
    in the torment of emotional distress,
when inwardly our hearts are screaming,
    though outwardly we smile,
as we break into fragments,
    are torn apart,
        disintegrate,
knowing separation from God,
    one another
        and within ourselves,
in all this the crucified resurrected One is there –
    at one –
at one with God
    with himself
        and with all humanity,
bringing healing in sickness,
    wholeness in brokenness –

For all shall be well
    and all shall be well
        and all manner of things shall be well.

*Pray with the Congregational Christian*
*Church in Samoa*
*(CWM Pacific Region).*

**Read**  Isaiah 50:4-9a; Psalm 70; Hebrews 12:1-3; John 13:21-32

We come to you, Jesus,
come humbly to your feet,
to dwell on you, in awe,
worship
and wonder.

We dwell on the majesty, devotion and integrity of who you are –
our Jesus, perfecter of our faith,
able to look towards the cross and set your face like flint,
in the midst of your betrayal, to be confident in your faithful God,
in the midst of insult and injury, to proclaim affirmation from God.

In the confident security of God keeping faith with you,
you accepted the cross, accepted betrayal,
disregarded humiliation and public shame.

You knew that if God promised to affirm
no one then could find you guilty.
You knew with God there is no fear of ultimate shame.

Jesus, you tell us that God does not shame, but glorifies,
God does not belittle, but raises up,
God does not condemn, but releases, welcomes, frees.

Jesus, you show us by being willing to listen and to hear,
we will always hear God's word of love for us,
God's word of courage, of hope, of renewal.

Jesus, you declare that shame and guilt may mark the path
but they are not its end.
Through you, who endured the cross,
we are promised a place of welcome at God's side.

## Wholeness in brokenness

In the chaos of war,
    in the violence of hatred
when the commonality of life
    is rent asunder,
as barriers are built
    based on difference of race or religion
creating camps of them and us,
in all this the crucified resurrected One is there –
    at one –
at one with God,
    with himself
        and with all humanity,
bringing love in disunity,
    wholeness in brokenness –

For all shall be well
    and all shall be well
        and all manner of things shall be well.

*Pray with the Presbyterian Church in
Taiwan (CWM East Asia Region).*

**Read** John 13:1-17, 31b-35

Is this how you will be glorified, Lord? By washing my feet?
Do you know what you are doing, stooping down that low?
You degrade yourself. You reduce your glory to sheer ordinariness.

A rather personal, embarrassing ordinariness.
I don't think about my feet much.
Nor the servant whose job it is to wash them:
this nobody, scrabbling about under the table,
removing dirt from between my toes,
whilst above him in the lamp-light we share our liberation meal
and talk about important things like the freedom of our people,
and the salvation of the world,
and grand gestures, and heroic betrayals.
Do you know what you are doing, becoming a nobody yourself?
If you are my Lord and Teacher,
I, too, am degraded; you are dragging me down as well.

Then let me learn the lessons of power and glory from below.
Enable me to see your presence amongst the nobodies and nameless ones.
Help me to serve you in the trivial round and common task.
Tell me again that ministry does not start with dynamic leadership
but with small, unnoticed things, and attention to detail,
like tying up a child's shoe and caring for an elderly relative.
Through my feet, teach me to walk your road.
Through the water, show me how you cleanse and heal and comfort.
Through the towel, let me know your gentle touch.

Bring me down, Lord, down to where glory must begin:
in loving service, in loving one another, in loving those who deny me,
in loving to the end.
Teach me to do for others what you have done for me.
And help me to know how simply I can be bathed in glory.

## Forsaken?

One day a man came into the chapel space absolutely distraught.
He beat his hands on the chair and stood right up in front of the Table,
crying openly in his distress, saying 'How can there be a God when my
little boy has a brain tumour'. Then turning to me, 'Just pray for him to
be made well'.

We sat down and I spoke gently of the trust he was showing even if he
didn't feel it, of how he sensed his need for God at this time, that this was
evident in his coming to meet with God somehow in this place, and of
my belief that God would be with him and his little boy throughout the
surgery and in all the times ahead. Then we prayed for calm and peace
and for God's healing touch to be with them all. Immediately he raced
back to the ward saying 'my son needs me with him'.

A day or two later the same man appeared in the chapel office asking
whether he could buy a Bible. We gave one to him and asked if we
could help in any way, but he simply wanted to read it for himself.
Later I visited his wife who was with their son, and other children
on the ward, and heard how they all were managing in this ordeal.
The little boy was doing well and so were they.

Days later this father asked for baptism for all the family in the hospital
chapel. By now their son was well enough to go home, so we talked
about the possibility of being part of a local church so there could
be thanksgiving and celebration in their own community for their
homecoming, and expression of faith in their service of baptism.
They liked this idea and wanted to be put in touch with a church near
to them and a minister who was pleased to help their whole family in
this step of faith and support them in future times. They went home in
good heart and with our prayers.

*Deborah McVey, a hospital chaplain*

*Pray for all who feel forsaken, for whatever reason.*

Good Friday – good God? How can we pray today?
Day of anguish and death, day of wretchedness and pain.
How can we pray today?
Day of sorrow, day of unbelief, day of questions.
Day with such sickening loss of hope.
How can we pray at all?

God, why are you so far away, why should my son suffer?
Why is my mother dying? Where are you now?
How can I pray today?
Why do you hide your face from us?
Why can't you hear my words of groaning?
How can we pray at all?

Good Friday – day of rejection, crucifixion, the worst death,
mocking crowds, no relief from pain, just passion and love,
Why did Jesus have to die today?
Why does anyone have to die today?
My tears cry to you both day and night
But you do not answer. I find no rest.
My God – I cannot pray.

*My child, know I am your God,*
*Be still and know . . . your cries of anguish are your prayers,*
*offered continually.  As Jesus offered his life for others, for wholeness,*
*for healing, so you, like him, offer yourself for others' well-being.*
*Believe me, I know your pain, I hold you in your grief.*
*Despite your sorrow you will be made whole, reshaped by suffering,*
*sure of my presence amidst unimaginable absence.*
*Out of your anguish you will see light.*

## The tidal wave

Days after the tsunami struck a group from the Cambridgeshire Ecumenical Council visited the Church of South India, staying within the Diocese in Vellore, with which they are partnered. It was a planned visit; amongst many events we were present at the opening of five new churches, two community centres and two schools, and we visited hospitals, hostels, special schools and support centres. The CSI is thriving and deeply involved with communities in towns and rural areas, especially with Dalit people who are still discriminated against when they convert to Christian faith.  Many people are poor but sacrificial giving is much in evidence.  A woman was honoured at one ceremony, 'she gave the money for the bell which calls people to prayer, even though she is poor', a pastor told us.  A gypsy colony (until conversion to Christianity still sacrificing bullocks and sheep) celebrated the opening of their new bamboo church with dancing and unaccompanied Tamil songs which were vibrant.  The women visitors were invited to light the ghee lamp before the prayer of dedication for the church.  Dancing, singing and feasting went with every celebration.

The community of Cuddalore, south of Pondicherry, was starting the recovery process from the tsunami.  Boats were still piled high like flotsam and there were gaping spaces where dwellings had been. Already new shelters with concrete walls and plastic sheeting for roofing were emerging in some of those spaces.  Ordinary life was continuing; lines of washing were all around us; the women and children still looked colourful and elegant in their sarees with fresh flowers in their hair, even amidst such disaster.  Unusually, there was no begging here; the people have immense dignity in their suffering and were simply pleased to see us and the pastors who hosted us. The CSI has been giving out of its slender resources people, possessions and money for relief work; up and down the coast the tent cities were dotted amongst the fields by the shoreline.  Our prayers and practical help are needed to ensure the CSI can continue this outreach and ministry in the name of Jesus Christ.

*Deborah McVey*

*Pray for the Church of South India (CWM South Asia Region).*

**Read**   Psalm 31:1-4, 15-16; 1 Peter 4:1-8; John 19:38-42

Hidden Jesus,
bind me in your passion,
hide me in your wounds,
death's darkness, I know,
pain of deep imagination.
I sorrow with you.

Utterly numb, heart and mind, no way out, body and spirit,
hopes dashed, smashed, fearful weeping, grievous grieving.

Heart-wrenching wretchedness, helpless helplessness,
terror-struck trembling, shaking, shivering despair.

Incarnation of Love,
gravely buried, petrified,
sealed with screaming sorrow,
the secret feel of crying shame.

Overwhelmingly engulfed,
swept away, drowned,
all-consuming tears.
untimely end of all things.

Unhopeful hoping,
no words forming,
just waiting, waiting
in speechless silence.

***God, why God, have you forgotten your people?***
***Lead us from this dark night into your place of light and life.***

*(this was influenced by the Holy Saturday human experience of the
tsunami disaster around the Indian Ocean, Christmas 2004)*

## Church of the living Christ

Church of the living Christ,
people of Easter faith –
speak to the Man who walks
free from the dark of death!
>       The Christ who burst the tomb apart
>       comes questioning the Church's heart.

No use old wineskins now –
new wine is here to stay:
no patching up old schemes –
new patches tear away,
>       old gear, old concepts have no place
>       where Christ's own presence sets the pace.

Women and men of God,
come, as one Church to serve,
bring all the skills we have,
sharpen our every nerve:
>       to save a world in bitter need
>       the rule of love must come in deed.

We are the Body now –
our feet must mark the Way,
our speech declare the Word
and live it day by day,
>       the resurrection story ours,
>       disciples gifted with new powers!

*Shirley Murray*
*This may be sung to the tune 'Little Cornard'*
*or other 66.66.88 tune*

*Pray with the Presbyterian Church of Aotearoa New Zealand*
*(CWM Pacific Region).*

# Praying with CWM churches

**Council for World Mission**
a global community of churches

# AFRICA

## Church of Jesus Christ in Madagascar (FJKM)

Much of Madagascar suffers poverty and unemployment, and the FJKM is seeking to respond to these problems. It runs 450 schools and recently began a project to fight bribery, HIV/AIDS and poverty.

Give thanks:
- For FJKM ministries, such as its orphanage and handicraft centre;
- For church life continuing despite the economic crisis and the difficulties faced by congregations and society as a whole.

Pray:
- For FJKM member boards in their decision making;
- For church ministries to succeed in their goals over the next four years;
- For state and funding bodies to work together effectively;
- For social and economic rebuilding.

© NICK SIREAU/CWM

*Passing time: A man strums in the shade in Marovoay, Madagascar. Poverty and unemployment are rife in the nation and the church is working to combat it.*

## Churches of Christ in Malawi (CCM)

Malawi is deeply in debt. There are high numbers of people with HIV/AIDS, and food production is hampered by frequent drought. The church supports Malawians with drought-relief and income-generating craft projects.

Give thanks:
- For the Christian witness despite economic and social hardship;
- For the leadership of general secretary Rev Goodwin Zainga.

Pray:
- For the constitution review process aimed at good governance in the CCM;
- For Malawi as it prepares itself for more food shortages. Rains stopped before the 2005 staple maize crop had matured.

## United Church of Zambia (UCZ)

The UCZ is concerned with issues of AIDS, increasing school drop-out rate, street youth, unemployment, delinquency and international debt.

Give thanks:
- For the Women of Substance project. The project educates women and encourages a lifestyle that will minimise the risk of reproductive ill health.

Pray:
- For the fight against HIV/AIDS and for those caring for patients with the disease;
- For missionaries to Zambia Sulota Drong, Alison Gibbs, Laya Mozumder, Aaron and Rose Naule, Brian and Georgina Payne, Marina Sarder, and Rev Fereti and Sosefina Tutuila.

*Toil: A woman does domestic chores with a baby on her back in Mwandi village, Zambia.*

# United Congregational Church of Southern Africa (UCCSA)

The UCCSA has congregations in Botswana, Mozambique, Namibia, South Africa and Zimbabwe. It works to combat violence, crime and poverty and addresses HIV/AIDS.

Give thanks:
- For successful and peaceful elections in Botswana, Mozambique, Namibia, South Africa and Zimbabwe;
- For a successful UCCSA ministers convention in January 2005;
- For a good rainy season in four of the countries in which the UCCSA serves.

Pray:
- For the election of a general secretary at the 2005 Assembly in South Africa;
- For the resolution of the drought and economic problems in Zimbabwe.


# Uniting Presbyterian Church in Southern Africa (UPCSA)

The UPCSA seeks to be one in obedience to the Lord, in celebrating diversity including its own cultural diversity, in addressing injustices and poverty and in providing a model of racial reconciliation. It is striving to prioritise evangelism, stewardship and its response to HIV/AIDS, focusing on widows and orphans.

Pray:
- That God may journey with the UPCSA in making its vision a reality;
- For the work of the UPCSA general secretary Rev Vuyani Vellem;
- For an end to the HIV/AIDS epidemic and for UPCSA congregations' strength and compassion as they care for those affected by the disease;
- For youth evangelism ministry development;
- For the training of ministers, lay people and elders;
- For the encouragement of women – both lay people and ministers.

---

*Front cover: A woman stands outside Trinity Congregational Church in Soweto, South Africa. Photo: © Kenwyn Pierce/CWM*

# CARIBBEAN

## Guyana Congregational Union (GCU)

Guyana suffers social and economic instability, causing many potential leaders to leave the country. This problem affects the church, which is battling to train and keep ministers.

Give thanks:
- For the church's youth and children's work;
- For its outreach during the floods in early 2005, providing aid and shelter.

Pray:
- That suitable people will respond to the call to serve as missionaries in the GCU;
- That mission programmes will successfully reach people;
- That the wider GCU membership would assist in the church restructuring process;
- For peaceful elections in Guyana in 2006 and that God's vision prevails.

© NNEOMA CHIMA/CWM

*Creative: Children perform at a church dance competition.*

## United Church in Jamaica and the Cayman Islands (UCJCI)

The United Church has as its theme United in Faith: A Caring Church in a Changing World. The UCJCI is responding to some of the care issues through its children's homes, ministry to young mothers and to AIDS patients.

Give thanks:
- For the launch of counselling care centres as places of refuge, healing and wholeness for persons with emotional crises;
- For the recovery efforts in Cayman and Jamaica after the devastation of Hurricane Ivan in 2004 and for the support of the UCJCI's partners.

Pray:
- For the new UCJCI general secretary, Rev Collin Cowan;
- For the ministry of missionary nurse to Haiti Joan Page Bain;
- For churches to be a healed and healing community in Cayman and Jamaica;
- That congregations will become more involved in creating peace and justice.

# EAST ASIA

## Gereja Presbyterian Malaysia (GPM)

The GPM run social projects among the Chinese in Malaysia. It is growing in membership and planting new fellowships in urban East Malaysia.

Give thanks:
- For the government support of interfaith dialogue;
- For church ministries to the disabled and drug addicts.

Pray:
- For religious freedom;
- For effective evangelism;
- For peaceful relations between different faiths in Malaysia;
- For ministries to women and youth.

## Hong Kong Council of the Church of Christ in China (HKCCCC)

The HKCCCC serves in all realms of social life – from schools to care of the elderly. It has voiced its concerns, alongside other Hong Kong churches, about issues relating to China's control of government of the island.

Give thanks:
- For the Hoh Fuk Tong redevelopment project, which will include rebuilding the existing secondary school, primary school, and retreat/conference centre, scheduled to finish within 10 years;
- For the reconciliatory political climate and the continued recovery of the economy.

Pray:
- For the former chief executive, who resigned suddenly, and for the change of leadership in the government;
- For the reorganisation of the government – that it will be able to care for the people of Hong Kong with wisdom and love;
- For the Bible study group programme, worship and spiritual renewal in the church;
- For the leadership and staff team to have health, wisdom and spiritual direction.

# Presbyterian Church in Singapore (PCS)

The Singapore government is encouraging the inflow of talents and funds to enhance economic growth and give space for the development of creativity and entrepreneurship. The PCS is concerned at the liberalisation of media, arts, entertainment and social permissiveness that has resulted out of this process.

Give thanks:
- For answered prayer in receiving two new full-time staff members at synod in 2005. Wilson Tan is a youth executive, and Lau Jen Sin is communications executive.

Pray:
- That congregations will rally behind the vision of the moderator's elect, Rev Phua Chee Seng, to double PCS membership by 2011;
- For the church's 125th anniversary celebration in April 2006; that it would bring church members together in worship and in fundraising for the plan to double membership;
- For the synod mission to develop a Presbyterian resource library at Trinity Theological College, a Presbyterian centre for Bible and social ministries and training conference centre, and a Presbyterian foundation to gather financial resources for synod development;
- That casinos will not be established in Singapore.

# Presbyterian Church in Taiwan (PCT)

The PCT is politically and socially active in Taiwan, strongly campaigning for the island's independence from China. It also has ambitious evangelistic targets and aims to draw 10,000 people to the Christian faith by 2005.

Give thanks:
- For the reunion of the Kaohsiung and Longevity Mountain presbyteries of the PCT, divided since 1972 over church planting and other issues.

Pray:
- For the new general secretary Rev Andrew Chang;
- For CWM missionary Carys Humphreys who is working in PCT administration;
- For more ministers to serve in aboriginal congregations;
- For the 21st century New Taiwan Mission Movement Project to increase membership by 10,000.

## Presbyterian Church of Korea (PCK)

The PCK is changing the emphasis of mission from growth in quantity to growth in quality – aiming for unity, peace, social service, justice and love.

Give thanks:
- For church growth and church ministries in Korean society;
- For the 2005 North and South Korean churches' worship service held during Easter at Mt Keum Kang.

Pray:
- For the peaceful reunification of North and South Korea;
- For the fruitful development of the Life Saving Movement for a Decade (2002 to 2012);
- For church mission to the unemployed, homeless, disabled, to foreign migrant workers and in hospitals, industrial areas, schools and prisons;
- For the empowerment of PCK youth.

*Accompaniment: A musician leads worship on a gayakum in Korea.*

## Presbyterian Church of Myanmar (PCM)

Myanmar struggles economically in the face of US and European sanctions. The church is battling to become financially self-reliant.

Give thanks:
- For the reopening of the Agape Clinic Hospital after four years' closure;
- For new believers in rural areas;
- For the successful gender awareness and leadership development programme.

Pray:
- For a resolution to the church's financial crisis;
- For the building of mission partnerships with overseas churches;
- For the printing press to be upgraded;
- That the church ordains women and that women take part in leadership;
- That the theological college is upgraded for a Master of Divinity programme.

# EUROPE

## Congregational Federation (CF)

The CF is seeking to help its congregations to grasp new opportunities for mission. Through its mission network coordinator new initiatives to support work among the elderly and an extension of youth and children's work have begun.

Give thanks:
- For new church initiatives at Cheadle, Truddoxhill, Cawsand and Dobcross;
- For the renewal process of the integrated training course;
- For those whose faithfulness and inspiration keep the gospel alive.

Pray:
- For local congregations to be ready to find new ways of being church;
- That younger people will offer themselves as leaders;
- That the church will take its place in the debate for justice and mercy in response to globalisation, trade, the environment, migration and asylum.

## Presbyterian Church of Wales (PCW)

The PCW has 775 churches throughout Wales, the majority with less than 50 members. It is restructuring, pursuing relationships with other churches, and developing new initiatives in witnessing to Christ and in service.

Give thanks:
- For a positive response to the training programme for leaders in mission;
- For the contribution of CWM missionaries from India, Singapore and Zambia;
- For the enthusiasm and support of women in all levels of the church.

Pray:
- That more young people will have a sense of calling to serve the gospel;
- For ongoing efforts to make the church's mission programme a success;
- For encouragement and a vision for the future among local congregations.

## Protestant Church in the Netherlands (PCN)

The PCN was formed in 2004 through the merger of Reformed and Lutheran churches. It seeks to proclaim Jesus to a society that is increasingly distancing itself from Christianity.

Give thanks:
- For church outreach to the disabled and the disadvantaged;
- For church work encouraging young Christians in their faith.

Pray:
- For a renewal of the Holy Spirit in the PCN;
- For peace between Muslim and non-Muslim sections of the Netherlands;
- For youth joining the Mission House in Amsterdam for 10 months.

## Union of Welsh Independents (UWI)

Most of the UWI's 500 churches use the Welsh language for business and worship. The union strives to defend and foster the language and culture, which are under threat. This generates a strong commitment to justice and empathy with others whose cultures are under pressure.

Give thanks:
- For the enthusiasm that surrounds the AGAPE programme for new vitality and relevance in mission;
- For all church members' unassuming faithfulness and perseverance;
- For leadership, insight and vision.

Pray:
- For the churches to be receptive to new training in order to serve more fully;
- For the ability to reach more young people and families with the gospel;
- For more deep faith in Jesus Christ.

## United Reformed Church (URC)

Many URC congregations are united with other denominations. It is reviewing its priorities to equip itself for mission in an increasingly secular society.

Give thanks:
- For ministry to prisoners, the homeless, asylum seekers and families.

Pray:
- For the success of the campaign to Make Poverty History;
- For wisdom in the Catch the Vision for God's Tomorrow review process;
- For the work of missionaries Rev and Mrs Chang Jen-ho, Henry and Maressa Iputau, Anjana and David Jonathan, and Hanitrarivo Raharimanana.

# PACIFIC

## Congregational Christian Church in American Samoa (CCCAS)
American Samoa is an incorporated territory of the US and many Samoans are serving the US military campaign in Iraq. The CCCAS especially seeks to minister to young people through its teaching. It is also planning to build a youth centre.

Give thanks:
- For 25 years of its mission and ministry;
- For the establishment of mission churches at military bases;
- For the development of a programme for theological education for women.

Pray:
- For local military reservists in places of world conflict;
- For more people to staff the church educational institutions;
- For wider church missionary opportunities for seminary students.

## Congregational Christian Church in Samoa (CCCS)
Samoa is a deeply conservative Christian society, but is increasingly influenced by secularism, materialism and individualism.

Pray:
- For work to combat HIV/AIDS and to deal with issues including suicide, drug abuse, diabetes and high blood pressure;
- For strengthening of church pastoral and teaching ministry;
- For church and society to maintain family, culture and community spirit;
- For missionaries from India, Vanlalthanpuii Chawngthu, Lalengzami Chhakchhuak, Zorinpuii Khiangte and Rachel Zote.

## Congregational Union of New Zealand (CUNZ)
The union encourages its members to help socially as well as spreading the message of Christianity.

Give thanks:
- For the new chairperson Peter Eccles;
- That in 2005 23,000 people, mostly aged 15 to 25, attended the Parachute Christian music festival.

Pray:
- That the general election in 2005 will result in the election of many members of parliament who uphold traditional Christian values and Christian marriage;
- For wisdom for the CUNZ leaders;
- For the youth of New Zealand and the youth in the CUNZ churches;
- That with the use of the Purpose Driven Church model congregations grow in fellowship, discipleship, worship, ministry and evangelism.

## Ekalesia Kelisiano Tuvalu (EKT)

The majority of Tuvalu belongs to the EKT. The church ministers to society through developing rural congregations, running a video library newsletter and a hospital, schools and maritime schools chaplaincy. Tuvalu faces the threat of HIV/AIDS and rising sea-levels due to global warming.

© JOCELYN CARLIN

Pray:
- For church wisdom in responding to the growing threat of HIV/AIDS;
- For solutions to the effects of global warming.

*Keeping watch: Rising sea levels threaten the future of Tuvalu.*

## Kiribati Protestant Church (KPC)

The KPC is in a Christian-dominated society. It is concerned with increasingly extreme weather, rising sea levels, erosion and loss of crops in island nations.

Pray:
- For church and nation to be given a voice at meetings discussing action on environmental degradation;

- For the youth and Sunday school activities;
- For CWM missionaries to Kiribati: Violet Jasmine Joseph, Bessie and Joseph Paineitala, Milton Ponnappan and R Rajendran;
- For Kiribati's response to HIV/AIDS;
- For church finances to carry out its mission and ministry.


## Nauru Congregational Church (NCC)

Seventy per cent of Nauruans belong to the NCC. The church, like all of Nauru, faces financial difficulty. Nauru's main source of industry – phosphates – are nearly depleted and the country needs new sources of income.

Pray:
- For its preparation of religious teaching for use in primary and high schools;
- For its plans to become self-sustaining financially;
- For new economic initiatives to develop the country;
- For church leaders in training.


## Presbyterian Church of Aotearoa New Zealand (PCANZ)

The PCANZ is mission focused – seeking to make a difference in society through social services and church programmes for youth, cultural groups, Christian basics courses and holiday programmes. Worship varies from traditional and formal to contemporary and informal.

Give thanks:
- For the 50th anniversary of the PCANZ Maori Synod Te Aka Puaho in 2005;
- For volunteers and church members that give their skills and gifts to the church's mission of making Jesus Christ known;
- For New Zealand's clean, green environment;
- For the contribution of PCANZ aid and development partner Christian World Service to relief efforts in tsunami-struck Indonesia, India and Sri Lanka and other parts of the world.

Pray:
- For the annual Connect conference, which brings together Presbyterian youth leaders for worship, sharing, fun and inspiration;
- That the PCANZ will build, maintain and renew partnerships with national and international churches and institutions;

- For the Kid's Friendly project to encourage and assist churches in ministering to children and families;
- For national mission enabler John Daniel, who works alongside congregations to help them with outreach in their communities.

## United Church in Papua New Guinea (UCPNG)

The vision of the UCPNG is to teach, preach and live the word of God in faith, life and witness, and in loving and caring ministries. Christianity is the main religion in Papua New Guinea.

Give thanks:
- For the launch of the first Mendi-language version of the New Testament.

Pray:
- For the church ministry to families, in particular its ministry to those suffering domestic violence;
- For peace among tribes in Papua New Guinea;
- For the UCPNG general secretary Rev Siulangi Kavora;
- For efforts to combat the spread of HIV/AIDS;
- For growth of compassion for people with HIV/AIDS.

## United Church in Solomon Islands (UCSI)

Several years of ethnic conflict in the Solomon Islands brought it to the brink of economic collapse. After peace was restored in 2003, the UCSI began ministries to boost local congregations and work towards financial self-reliance.

Give thanks:
- For an end to violence in the Solomon Islands;
- For the launch of a translation of the New Testament into Luqa in July 2004.

Pray:
- For church workshops and meetings to promote peace and reconciliation between different ethnic groupings in the Solomon Islands;
- For those seeking to avert an AIDS epidemic in the Solomon Islands;
- For a good working relationship between the Australian peace-keeping forces and Solomon Islanders.

# SOUTH ASIA

## Church of Bangladesh (CoB)

The CoB is a united church of 16,000 people. It serves in a Muslim-majority country where around 85 per cent of the population struggles for survival. The CoB reaches out through social action, irrespective of gender, caste or religion.

Give thanks:
- For all the support received from around the world during the flood in 2004, which caused such immense suffering for Bangladesh;
- For the work that is developing among very poor women and children.

Pray:
- For the future of Bangladesh, which suffers political turmoil and violence;
- For the church to grow and develop in order to meet people's needs, especially the young.

## Church of North India (CNI)

The church has over one million members and is striving to strengthen its parishes and dioceses to empower communities.

Give thanks:
- For the unity, witness and service of the church in all its areas of work: children's ministry, tribal and Dalit issues, promoting social consciousness and fighting against the stigma of HIV/AIDS.

Pray:
- For continued church unity and witness;
- For preparations for the 12th CNI synod in 2005 to plan for its future;
- For the July 2005 mission conference where leaders will plan mission to areas untouched by the gospel;
- For the continuing rehabilitation work in the Andaman and Nicobar Islands following the tsunami disaster.

*Raising awareness: An AIDS campaign poster in India.*

# Church of South India (CSI)

The CSI is active in political and social issues, especially in raising awareness of discrimination against girls. It focuses on evangelism to Dalits, who are looked down on in society because they are excluded from the Hindu caste system.

Give thanks:
- For the Total Heart Care Clinic at CSI Kalyani Hospital in Chennai;
- For the CSI Bishop Sargent School that provides education and job training for children with disabilities.

Pray:
- For fishing and other communities as they rebuild following the tsunami in December 2004;
- For peaceful interfaith relations;
- For religious freedom to be upheld;
- For equal rights for Dalits and girls.

# Presbyterian Church of India (PCI)

The PCI comprises of different North East Indian tribes. The church has about 1,000,000 family members, 2,500 churches, 650 ministers, and over 1,300 mission field workers.

Give thanks:
- For God's blessings and for his guidance;
- For the growth of the church and for unity among the PCI's seven synods.

Pray:
- For the peace initiatives taken by the PCI to restore peace normality and peaceful settlement in conflict areas. Kidnapping, banditry and insurgency are rife in north-eastern India;
- For displaced people affected by violence;
- For the PCI secretariat and other units as they prepare for the revival centenary celebration in 2006 at the Presbyterian Church Mairang in Meghalaya, an area bordering Bangladesh.

Council for World Mission, Ipalo House, 32-34 Great Peter Street, London SW1P 2DB, UK
Tel: +44 (0)20 7222 4214    Fax: +44 (0)20 7233 1747 or +44 (0)20 7222 3510
Email: council@cwmission.org.uk    Website: www.cwmission.org.uk
Registered Charity No 1097842    Company No 4758640    Registered in England and Wales
Printed by Healeys Printers, Ipswich, UK

**Read**  Psalm 118:1-2, 14-24; John 20:1-18

Day's beginning, sleep done, though not too well,
for memory of past sorrows crowd in.
This is a new day, day of new beginnings,
holding to past times, reshaping towards a future.

*And then for sure – God is with us!*
**I shall not die – but I shall live!**

The longest night has cleared away, and with it doubts and fears,
for with the dark has gone the stone,
the grave holds no one in its grasp,
for Christ is risen, he is not here.

**I shall not die – but I shall live!**

Give thanks my heart, that he's alive,
give thanks my soul, no more we grieve,
give thanks my mind, for answered prayer,
give thanks my strength, for Christ is here.

**I shall not die – but I shall live!**

Give thanks my all, for God is good,
with faithfulness that shakes the skies
and rocks the earth in rescuing us –
for Christ is risen, he's everywhere.

**We shall not die – but we shall live!**

## Awakening a new dawn

"This was where I was taken off the bus to be killed by Idi Amin's troops". As the Christian Aid team in Uganda crossed the Owens Falls Dam, their guide, Abraham Hodoto spoke about his experiences during that dark time in Uganda's history, when dissidents became bodies floating in the Nile. An incident at the far end of the bridge distracted Abraham's captors, and he ran for his life. Twenty years later, he personifies a new situation, in which he believes there is good news in Africa, and change is possible.

Christine Lubaale is a widow, looking after 13 children, 8 of whom are her own. Beside her small house she cultivates maize, cassava, beans, paw-paw, avocado, even some coffee. She is at the far end of a long and winding road called International Debt Cancellation. She is the human face that smiles or cries when political and economic decisions made in far-away summit meetings finally touch the earth. She sees the difference when Uganda's Poverty Action Fund money consistently improves roads, drills wells and builds new schools and local health clinics. Debt relief is changing her community.
Christine says, "we had much diarrhoea and ill health because of dirty water, but now we have a bore-hole which gives us clean water, and now all my children go to our newly built school".

Similar improvements can be seen throughout Uganda, with over seven million more children in school as a result of debt cancellation. Roads, clinics and bore-holes have multiplied.
Uganda is living proof that a new dawn can come, dispelling the darkness of global injustice.

*Pray that the pressure for debt cancellation for every indebted country will succeed.*

**Read**   1 John 1:1-4; John 20:19-31; Isaiah 65:17-25

God of Certainty,
how graceful and merciful you are.
You sent your Son who gave his life for us,
yet how suspecting and unsure we are.

As Thomas, as intellectuals, we suspected you.
As human beings, who have got everything by your grace,
we suspected you.

We doubt if you actually came.
We doubt if you actually died.
We doubt if you actually rose again.
We doubt if you ascended into heaven.
We doubt if you actually exist.

We do so because our human minds have limitations.
But we thank you for being the God of dialogue.
You offer space for us to have conversations.

So we offer our doubts and our suspicions not only about you,
but about ourselves, our world, our neighbours, the church.

Grant us serenity of thought and mind; so we may act with faith,
faith in your promises, faith in your vision,
for a world of new heaven and new earth,
where none shall labour in vain,
and there is no suffering and no pain.

## Jesus speaks my language

Situated between Benin and Ghana in West Africa, Togo is home to thousands of children who are suffering because of severe poverty. The Bible Society of Togo is making it a top priority to working with these children to offer them and their country hope for the future. So, portions of scripture are being distributed at sporting events; drama is being used to convey messages that will touch the lives of young people; and 'Faith comes by Hearing' audio tapes are used in schools, where as often as not enthusiastic head teachers bring in their own cassette players so the children can listen. Also these audio scriptures are having an impact on many adults, when non-Christian friends are invited along to the listening sessions, and some of them are now very much part of the church.

People were surprised to know that Jesus speaks Kabye (the local language), and they said that as Jesus speaks Kabye, it means he knows them: 'we feel like Jesus is talking to us directly'.

In the same way, there was tremendous excitement among the Sgaw Karen people in Myanmar when the Bible was published in their language recently, and in the Guarani tongue, in Bolivia, and in the Ngbaka language in the former Zaire.

Each group are now able to say,' We have the Bible in our own heart language, so God speaks clearly and directly to us. It is like Christ himself has come to visit us'.

Over 6,500 languages are spoken in the world. 414 have a complete Bible, and some 2,355 have some form of scripture (Summer 2004 figures). There are over 600 translation projects running at a time, and the Bible Society encourages and supports local translators who often spend years and even decades on a translation.

*Pray for the work of the United Bible Societies throughout the world (www.biblesociety.org.uk).*

# We believe

## Read   Luke 24:36b-48

You stand among us,
  calm centre in the storm,
  saying 'Peace be with you'.
Our hearts race, our knees knock,
  we check our glasses.

**We believe; help our unbelief.**

You hold out hands
  scarred by others' fear,
  point out feet still bleeding from others' failures,
and say it again:
 'Peace be with you'.

**We believe; help our unbelief.**

You sit among us,
  eat and drink,
  spit out bones
and laugh at our nervous jokes.
  You are here.

**We believe; help our unbelief.**

You open to us the word of truth,
  confirming what our hearts hunger to know,
  transforming fear to wonder,
and inviting us into speech.

**Risen Lord, be the breath in our words of witness.**
**As we believe, by your power may we proclaim.**

## A touch of hope

Tourists are now returning to the beaches of Croatia, so people in the UK ask, 'Why do we need reconciliation work there?'. Everything seems normal, and indeed it is, apart from Eastern Slavonia. Here people are still recovering from the onslaught by the Yugoslavian National Army on Osijek and Vukovar in 1991. In this region, with Hungary to the north, and Serbia to the east, many thousands of people still bear the scars of war. Whilst physical reconstruction is taking place, the emotional wounds take longer to heal.

The 'Touch of Hope' project is a co-operation between the Community for Reconciliation in Bromsgrove, near Birmingham, and the Centre for Peace, Non-Violence and Human Rights in Osijek. The project's goal is to heal the hurts of war and to work together for a healthy society, where there is equal opportunity for all regardless of ethnicity. It works from conflict to reconciliation.

Croatia is mainly a Catholic country, but the project works with members of all the denominations there – Roman Catholic, Serbian Orthodox, and Hungarian Reformed. Some do not profess any faith. Participants of workshops experience healing themselves, and act as channels of healing in their own communities. Consequently there is a ripple effect of change taking place in this war-torn country. Participants include key community figures, such as teachers, leaders of war veterans' associations, church workers, and youth leaders. The workshops, which last for one year, offer a 'safe' place where raw feelings can be expressed. Participants can begin to see how healing processes work and how shattered communities can be rebuilt. One participant said that being on the programme ' has restored her faith in human beings and also in God'. Change is possible in even the darkest of places.

*Clive Fowle*

*Pray with the Reformed Church in Croatia, which has links with the East Midlands Synod, and for the work of the Community for Reconciliation.*

# Just like sheep!

## Read    Psalm 23; Zechariah 10

Father God,
in towns and cities and even in villages,
we don't understand shepherding.
The people of Israel *knew* about flocks,
and about caring for them.
We know best about following the herd,
being identical to everyone else!
So, just as you shepherded Israel on their journeys
keep us on your path, and bring us home.

Lord Jesus,
you called yourself the Good Shepherd
when you spoke to those you called your sheep,
with their woolly thinking,
and their instinctive following of the biggest,
the loudest or the strongest.
When we follow the ways of the world like sheep,
set out and find us, and keep us in your love.
For we know that it is your love that calls us.

Thank you for loving us so much
that you were willing to show us how to be part of your flock
by becoming the Lamb of God yourself.
Thank you for risking yourself by trusting us to shepherd for you.
Thank you for giving us the love
that might one day lead others onto your path.

Lamb of God,
good shepherd,
enfold us in your arms,
and bring us safely home
at the end of every day.

## Christian Aid Week

Roseline runs the Vidyal  (meaning 'dawn') bank in Nachikuvichi, in
Tamil Nadu in South India.  These banks were suggested by workers
with the Christian Aid partner organisation Activists for Social
Alternatives (ASA) in 1990, and now there are 68,000 female members
of banks like Vidyal throughout Tamil Nadu, helping the women
become self-sufficient.  At 7.30am every Friday Roseline gathers the
women and collects their payments.  She explains how much the group
has helped to increase her self-esteem.
'At first, when we had a meeting, I was afraid to say my name.  Now,
I am the group leader and I have to speak a lot.  Everyone in the
village knows me now.  Together we had the guts to meet the leader
of the local council and have asked them to provide a water tap and
underground drainage to improve hygiene'.

When Roseline got married, life was hard.  Her husband Paulraj worked
as a night watchman and earned 400 rupees (£5) a month.  Roseline
joined ASA and gave him her first loan of 3,000 rupees to enable him to
start a painting business.  He got 20,000 rupees profit from the first job
and now employs 20 full-time staff.

The Vidyal bank has reduced people's dependency on loan sharks, who
used to charge nearly 15% interest over two months.  People no longer
ask for their assistance because they know about ASA.  The members of
these banks know that caste and gender will no longer hold them back.
They support each other as they strive to improve the lives of their
communities.  It is an example of how partnership, the bedrock
of Christian Aid, can really make a difference.

*Pray for the work of Christian Aid and the success of its fundraising
this week.*

# Speak out for those who cannot speak

s 5

**Read**   I John 4:7-21; Proverbs 31:8-9

O God of justice, lead us into the path of peace.
Forgive us when we ignore the less privileged.
Forgive us when we close our minds to see the privileges we have.
Forgive us when we liaise with the oppressors for our own benefit.
Forgive us when we close our hearts to the cries of the oppressed.

Give us your passion to forgive others who have acted against us.
Give us your compassion to care for the poor and the oppressed.
Give us your love to care for everyone as ourselves.

Help us to be part of the revolution to change the world:
> to fight against the exploitation of farmers,
> to fight against child labour,
> to fight against racial injustice,
> to fight against patriarchy,
> to fight against unjust trade,
> to work for unity and for peace and justice.

'Speak out for those who cannot speak, for the rights of all the destitute.
Speak out, judge righteously, defend the rights of the poor and needy'

*(Proverbs 31:8-9).*

## Discerning God's hand

Contemplative prayer is receptive prayer. In this way of praying we hold ourselves still before God and wait for what he has to give us. It is not a matter of telling God what we want but of allowing God to give us what he wants. There is of course a place for making our desires known to God: but in silent prayer we move beyond that into a simple readiness to receive.

Contemplative prayer gives birth to the contemplative life. Being a contemplative means being open to what comes; being ready to perceive God in whatever is happening to us and around us, and to receive whatever he may give us through what is happening. The events and situations that confront us all bring us something of God. Some call us to penitence, some require our patience, some evoke our compassion. Even the dark, unpleasant things show signs of his hand. In all these we can look for some token of God's presence or some beckoning of his hand.

Contemplative living means not spending our energy trying to control situations or events to suit ourselves, not being frustrated because things haven't gone the way we would like, but accepting what happens around us as something through which God is acting or speaking.

That does not mean, of course, that everything that happens is good, or that it is all God's doing; or that we should simply be passive victims of what is done to us. But it does mean that we can look for the hand of God even in the hard, unpleasant and frustrating things, and say 'Yes' to his working. Nor does it mean that we should be careless of the evils around us, or that we should do nothing to amend things that are wrong. Often one of the most difficult things to accept is ourselves. But paradoxically it is when we accept ourselves as we are with all our inadequacies and failures, when we look away from ourselves and focus instead on God, that God works his changes within us.

*Sandy Ryrie*

*Pray with the Kiribati Protestant Church (CWM Pacific Region).*

# To be in love

## Read   John 15:9-17

Lord, I feel like Peter –
for I can hear your question, 'Do you love me?'
and I say 'Lord, you know I love you',
yet with each reply I feel my affirmation shrink
and know you know I 'love' you as best I can.

You love me, and call me friend, not servant,
yet I hear your wishes as burdensome commands.
I am not motivated by a heart of love and care,
and find no joy in the fulfilment of your wishes.
You confide in me your heart's desires
and I say 'do I have to?'.

Living in love, abiding in love, is what it's all about.
It sounds sublime, but seems so hard.
Love cares, trusts, risks, attends,
never ends, and never gives up.
When love is genuine, the evidence of love is there for all to see.

How shall I love you more?
How shall I grow from 'love' to LOVE?

And you say
'Live with me, laugh with me, look through my eyes.
Don't struggle, don't fight, just be.
Don't think you always have to be better,
don't think 'never good enough' is you.
Let ME love YOU, (because I do),
and love will seed, and grow.'

Thank you for your love, Lord.
Thank you for your Love.

## Why do you stand there looking up?

Of *course* we stood there, looking toward heaven!
What else could we do?
We were earthbound, left forlorn in a world of shattered dreams.
And you, our Lord and Saviour, rose above it all –
above the floods that overwhelm, the beasts that crush the earth,
the evil and the righteous conquerors who think they alone are right.
What else could we do but look up to you,
and wrap you in two thousand years of glory?

Then remind us that on earth you never were so distant,
but the one with whom we ate and laughed and walked.
Even at your rising.  Slipping in amongst us.
Wounded by the world you had tried to love.
Remind us that you did not ask us to stand and gaze at heaven.
But to go back to the city.  To go out to the nations.
To carry on where you left off.

So help us to still be ourselves – with you, with everyone.
To start where we are: witnesses of your humility and our truth.
To be more interested in the job before us than the sky above.
To find more glory in serving than dominating,
in engaging than escaping.
Help us see that being lifted up and removed from our sight
was your way of giving us permission to get on with your work;
and that getting on with your work may be our way of finding you again.
Show us how, when we find and follow you in the here and now,
we are already being led into your eternity.
And how, when we stay with things that drag us down,
we may experience you lifting us up.
And how, when we are cannot hold you in our sight and understanding,
you can still touch us, and hold us,
and wrap us in your glory.

*Pray with the Protestant Church in the Netherlands (CWM Europe Region).*

# The kite

Read Luke 24:44-53; Acts 1:1-11

The kite soared and spun and swooped beneath the clouds,
snaking its tail, rattling against the wind,
now diving earthwards, brushing the ground,
now climbing the heavens
to set them alight with a flash of scarlet gold.

Who was holding it?
Strings barely visible, it seemed to have a life of its own.
Ah, there!   At the other side of the heath!
A couple, dwarfed by distance, drab by contrast,
stood transfixed and rooted to the spot,
totally absorbed in their kite flying.

But no, they were not small or motionless or drab.
They were not down there on the ground.
They were racing through the heavens in reckless celebration,
connected not by strings but by their utter concentration,
by their joy and by their passion.

Today, ascendant Jesus, let it be that way for us!
Small and earthbound though we are,
let us rise with you and dance across the sky,
connected not by strings but grace; by unconditional love.

Lift our hearts today, in spite of all that weighs us down.
Lift our lives above the flood of overwhelming odds.
Lift our eyes to meet the eyes of others,
to see a broader vision,
to walk with lighter step upon the earth, upon their dreams.
Lift us till we start to lift the hearts of those around us.
Catch us in your rising and the wild wind of your Spirit,
till we become like you: a kite for all the world.

## Finding the way

May 2004 saw the long-awaited enlargement of the European Union, and the Czech Republic's accession to it.  The churches, like the rest of society, are having to prepare for the new situation that EU membership has brought.  After the fall of communism in 1989 the churches continued to receive a degree of financial support from the state, but this is finally being phased out and the churches will have to find new means of funding their activities.  Like other churches, the main Protestant church, the Church of the Czech Brethren, has had to find new ways of raising money, and each congregation is being asked to raise a certain sum for church funds.  The church's ruling body, the Synodical Council (or Synodni Rada), made up of three clergy and three lay people, has a new team in place to face up to the new demands.  Pray for them, and for the outgoing team which guided the church through most of the difficult post-communist period.

They face social as well as economic change.  The development of market conditions has encouraged the spread of unwelcome phenomena like pornography.  And there is still tension between some Czechs and members of the large Roma (Gypsy) and Vietnamese communities.  A bewildering array of religious sects arrived from abroad in the first post-communist years, many of which made little effort to fit in with the established churches.  And the Czech Republic has become to some degree a 'staging post' for asylum seekers hoping to go on to Western Europe.  On many of these issues the church has a markedly different view from the rest of society, and needs courage to express it.

On the positive side, Czech Christians have welcomed the new opportunities to meet and co-operate with Christians from abroad. There has been a healthy increase in the number of young people studying at the theological faculty at Prague's Charles University, with a high percentage, over 50%, going on to become ministers.

*Malcolm Haslett*

*Pray with the Evangelical Church of the Czech Brethren, twinned with the Thames North Synod.*

**Read**  Acts 1:13-17, 21-26; John 17:6-19

We feel for your first ones, Jesus:
so privileged to be close to you in those heady, hectic years -
sharing your thoughts, lapping up your words, witnessing wonders.
Brave, hopeful years! Taking on the world as if there was no tomorrow.

Then suddenly – nothing. On their own. Unprotected.
No one showing them how, or doing it for them, or bailing them out.
No one coming back again, risen, undestroyed.
You had gone. And now you meant it.
And though future generations would glorify your going,
for your friends it was over. The final bereavement. The last straw.

So there they were – caught between a lost past and a hidden future,
between your mastery and their incompetence,
between an unexplained parting and an unknown Pentecost.
In no man's land. In the world but not of it.
In a world to which they did not now belong.

The eleven, their ineptitude exposed.
The twelfth: now the enemy – of them, of you, of life.
The one who took his place, but missed it all to inherit a confusion.
And the one who was not chosen.
We feel for your first ones, suddenly alone.

For we, too, know the moment when hopefulness goes sour;
when those we idolise leave, or let us down;
when those who lead the way press the reins into our hands;
when things that once were clear make no sense.

So tell us, loving Jesus, if in some way you are here –
tell us once again that we are not alone,
but held in prayer by you, and sanctified by truth.

## Spirit of peace

Wind of God, blow strongly,
break the walls of hate,
sweep away divisions;
open wide love's gate.
Heal and cleanse and strengthen
hearts that still are cold
and, in every language,
let your truth be told.

Harmonising Spirit,
spread your flame of peace –
burning brighter, stronger,
light of love increase.
Fill with warmth and brightness
every darkened place.
Let your joy and radiance
shine on every face.

Gentle, dove-like Spirit,
soothing frightened hearts,
strengthen and encourage
till all fear departs.
Then strong cries for justice
will at last be heard;
ears, long closed, will listen,
by these voices stirred.

Come then, lively Spirit,
fill this world of pain,
end the reign of violence,
set us free again …
Free from all oppression,
let the fighting cease;
enmity behind us,
build your world of peace.

*Wendy Ross-Barker*

## We shall dream dreams

**Read**    Ezekiel 37:1-14; Acts 2:1-21

Immortal God,
mortals you made us and life evades us.

But you are immortal and such is your might
that you bring hope and sight.

Renew our vigour,
pour out your spirit and give us new light.

We shall dream dreams,
with joy we shall scream,
looking around,
people sing praises, in diverse phrases,
languages and music, colours and faces.

We shall dream dreams,
with joy we shall scream,
thank you and thank you, Spirit divine,
stronger addiction is this than the wine.

We shall dream dreams,
with joy we shall scream,
blessed be your name
that never leaves us same.

Isaiah 6:1-8<br>Psalm 29<br>Romans 8:12-17<br>John 3:1-17

## God on the airwaves

Madagascar is changing fast. It has a fresh government committed to sustainable and rapid development. The nation is pushing its resources into education, disease prevention (especially HIV/AIDS), restoring the infrastructure such as roads, and fighting corruption.

The Church of Jesus Christ in Madagascar (FJKM) wants to be at the forefront of the regeneration. The FJKM has ambitious plans for the nation, setting up social development programmes and activities. To do this it needs to ensure that all members of the church share the same vision and are committed to the same goals. But with over 3 million members across the country, and little more than 1,000 ministers, getting news to members is a difficult and drawn out process, and written material is not the answer.

So, to combat the problem, the church is to extend and develop its radio station. Radio Fahazavana (Radio Light) has broadcast to Antananarivo, the capital, since 1997. The station is church-run and church-led, with the content mainly religious, cultural and social broadcasting.

There is also an educational content, guiding the listeners with information about how to prevent the spread of disease by hygiene, and how to treat illnesses. It also tackles such issues as degradation of the environment, and fighting corruption.

Now, with CWM's Mission Programme Support allocation, there are plans to set up five regional stations, which will reach the whole population. The hope is to unite the church and the nation in common goals for the good of the whole nation.

*Pray with the Church of Jesus Christ in Madagascar (CWM Africa Region).*

# Three-in-one-God, you are Holy

**Read**    Isaiah 6:1-8; Romans 8:12-17; John 3:1-17

Creating One, maker of heaven and earthly things,
your presence fills the whole universe.
You are high above the immensity of creation,
yet close as the blood that pulses through our bodies
and the breath that gives new life in each moment.

**In this season of the Spirit, draw us closer, Holy God,
so that we, your children, grow together in your kingdom.**

Rescuing One, bringer of healing and of peace,
your presence inspires faith in heavenly things.
You challenge our belief and commitment,
yet love us beyond all limits, forgiving everything
and holding before us the perspective of eternity.

**In this season of the Spirit, draw us closer, Holy Jesus,
so that we, your children, grow together in your kingdom.**

Sustaining One, nurturing and refreshing our spirits,
your presence fills us with life and strength for the day.
You fill us with dreams and enable us to fly,
yet comfort us when we fall, inspire us anew
and lift us to the throne of grace in love and acceptance.

**In this season of the Spirit, draw us closer, Holy Spirit,
so that we, your children, grow together in your kingdom.**

**Ever present three-in-one God, you are Holy.
May we know you in water, wind and fire, and in Jesus Christ,
that in knowing you we may become inheritors of eternal life.**

## The sound of silence

How loud the world is when we are silent.
I had forgotten how a gentle breeze could sing:
or how the birds are like a choir,
each adding a note to the harmony.
Leaves rustle as they fall,
spiralling down from tree top to ground
and the Abbey stones hum
with remembered prayers and holy joy.

How loud everything is when we are silent.
Spoons on china, feet on gravel paths,
the closing of a door, opening of a window,
taps running.
Familiar sounds heard freshly magnified.
And in our heads words
of remembered prayers and holy joy.

There is no need for speech when we are silent.
A glance, a gesture, eye contact, a smile,
says enough.
We hear.
We hear beyond speech
to resonance and stillness
of God's creation,
as in our heads he speaks
in remembered prayers and holy joy.

*Barbara Bennett*

*Pray for those who will be experiencing silence on this Nationwide Quiet Weekend, and for all those who will be ministering to them, physically and spiritually.*

# From small beginnings the kingdom grows

## Pentecost 2

**Read**    1 Samuel 16:11-13; Mark 4:30-34

Lord God,
you choose us in many ways,
breaking into our familiar tasks,
and everyday routine.
Shattering our complacency
and self-centredness,
you empower us by your Spirit
to do whatever you need us to do.

Lord,
remind us of the mustard seed
when we deny our own ability.
When *we* feel too small
and too inadequate to be useful,
help us to make space and silence
for you to speak to us.
Lord, make us aware
of the strengths that *you* can see in us.
Make us listen and obey,
for you will not leave us unprepared
or unable to fulfil the tasks of your Kingdom.

As you spoke to David,
the shepherd boy who became a king;
as you spoke through psalmist and prophet,
and in the words of Jesus,
so speak to us in the silence of our hearts,
and give us the grace to accept your will,
to receive your gifts,
and to serve you in love.

**25 June**

1 Samuel 17:(1a, 4-11, 19-23) 32-49
Psalm 9:9-20 or 1 Samuel 17:57-18:5, 10-16
Psalm 133
2 Corinthians 6:1-13
Mark 4:35-41

## The five stones of agape  *(Read 1 Samuel 17:1-51)*

The Union of Welsh Independents (UWI) is starting a three-year venture to revitalise its churches in 2005.  The Agape project aims to boost churches through advice and training on mission and ministry.  UWI general secretary Revd Dewi Hughes said: 'The programme seeks to engender a positive attitude in churches, to encourage a spirit of hope and adventure.  Often the decline in vitality has been so sharp that churches need to recapture the gospel vision for worship and outreach'.

Agape enabler Revd Meirion Morris of the Presbyterian Church of Wales will work alongside churches to help see how to best develop their mission.  Training co-ordinator for south Wales UWI minister Revd Dr Noel Davis will promote training for church leaders and members and oversee training for the ministry.  He will work in partnership with the existing training officer in north Wales, Euros Wyn-Jones.  Dr Davis said he especially wants to boost interdenominational training in the Welsh-speaking UWI.  'A tremendous amount of collaboration is already happening in English language training in Cardiff, south Wales, but we are trying to collaborate on Welsh language training'.

The project has £220,000 at its disposal to fund new mission ideas or training.  Mission ideas already suggested by churches have been school homework classes, or a lunch or tea for the elderly.

AGAPE stands for the Welsh words Addysg, Gweinidogaeth, Arweinyddiaeth, Prosiectau, Effeithiolrwydd – Education, Ministry, Leadership, Projects, Effectiveness.

*Pray with the Union of Welsh Independents, as they meet at their Annual Assembly from 29th June-1st July.*

**Read** Mark 4:35-41

God of motion, God of life,
God of journeying, with all its strife,
all life's hassles, all its big storms,
could not stop you reaching the other side.

As we travel now, into and through this world,
the boats of our lives seem to be whirled.
So we have stopped journeying, as we should.
We have become stagnant, in this changing world.

We have built churches, and spiritual castles
to keep us safe.
Wake us up! Rebuke our sleep! And then please persist
to help us say to wrestling world, 'Peace! Be Still!'.
With faith in you, hear our prayer, this we, Lord, insist.

## Catching the vision

St Andrew's URC in Leeds has turned its rooms into 'Martha and Mary's Bed and Breakfast' and 'Solomon's Temple' for a new method of Sunday school teaching. It is laying the foundations for the Workshop Rotation Model (Worm) of teaching, which aims to make the Sunday school venue a place that stimulates children's imaginations. It also uses computers, models, puppets, drama, songs, poems, puzzles and games to help young people learn. A design team at St Andrew's has turned one room into a Bedouin tent with an easy-to-assemble awning.

Eventually there will be four different workshops run on rotation for children aged three up to school Year two (usually ages five to six), and for children from Year 3 to 13. The team hopes after five years to have developed a core curriculum of teaching that can be repeated on a five-yearly rotation, which it will share with other churches.

One of advantage of Worm is that many different people can be involved; teaching an individual workshop, for example, or helping with puppets or drama. More information can be found at www.rotation.org.

St Mark's United Reformed Church in Wythenshawe, in Manchester, hosts an imaginative 'Tree of Life' project, where members of the local community can have access to massage and reflexology, and classes in healthy cooking, computing, home decoration, and fitness. These initiatives occur alongside more predictable community initiatives like a credit union and a low-cost home goods store. Future plans are to extend the project to provide a community café, and to deepen support for people with mental health problems. St Mark's has given up their church hall and a large part of their worship area to the project, which is run by about 60 volunteers, both from church and community.

*Pray for the United Reformed Church as it meets in General Assembly from 7th-10th July in Exeter.*

God, grant us the grace
   to welcome interruptions,
   to recognise the tugged sleeve as an opportunity,
   to be willing to stop even worthwhile tasks
   when your urgent business presses in.

Give us eyes to see and ears to hear
   the pain you wish us to address.
Then give us the will to respond
   with the tender patience you offered
   to those who pressed in on you.

Help us to see our abundance, also,
   as an opportunity to meet another's need.
Give us glad and generous hearts
   to play our part
   in the fair balance of the divine economy.

Calm our fear.
Strengthen our faith.
Complete the good work you have begun in us.

## Sharing in practice

Rev Hmar Sangkhuma, from the Presbyterian Church of India, is working for the Presbyterian Church of Wales at the moment. He has volunteered to help run the youth club in the town of Nantyffyllon, and this is giving him opportunities to share the gospel. Not only does he speak to the young people about his faith, but he invites them to join the Sunday School at the Trinity Presbyterian Church next door. He has also started visiting the local primary and comprehensive schools, which helps to build friendships with the young people at the club.

At the club the children play games or sports, listen to music, learn to dance, or sit and talk. Organisers are planning to introduce a computer skills course to help the children with their studies. They are also aware that those children who come from one-parent families especially need to develop life skills, and Hmar is helping in all these respects.

*Pray with the Presbyterian Church of Wales, meeting in General Assembly from 10th-13th July (CWM European Region).*

# Gifts of glory

**Read**  2 Samuel 5:1-5, 9-10; Psalm 48; 2 Corinthians 12:2-10; Mark 6:1-13

Lord God,
when other people come to us, and invite us
to use our skills for them,
save us from feeling too important and proud.

Lord God,
when we are tempted to meditate
upon our own progress and achievements,
remind us that it is your glory we should contemplate.

Lord God,
when we are sent out to be your people,
without any tools in our hands except your Word,
give us words and actions that will set the world aflame.

Lord God,
do not allow us to be foolish in thought, word or deed,
unless we make fools of ourselves for you,
for you are strength in our weakness.

*So we offer all that we do,*
*all that we have,*
*all that we are*
*to your glory, Lord.*
*For you give us our abilities,*
*build up our skills,*
*and offer us the words and strength*
*to be your people in the world.*

## Better together

Normandy – autumn leaves, cows lowing, a little château with pinnacles punctuating the mist, flax swathed around the walls of the barn, apple tarts and cake, a buzz of conversation, smiling attentiveness, cups of hot cider at the end of the day.   A regional synod of the Eglise Réformée de France is in full swing.  Didier speaks of mission in Africa, Dany of distance learning.  Frédéric pleads for destitute asylum-seekers; Hélène talks of the spiritual needs of young people.

The major theme of the Church in 2005 is this: How are we to confess Jesus Christ in a secular society?  Five priorities are identified: Mission; Nurture and Catechesis; Worship; Youth Work; World Church (including the Colloque franco-britannique and relations with the Wessex Synod of the United Reformed Church). Task groups are set up to further the work in each area.

How then to facilitate the proclamation of the Gospel and enable more effective fellowship between churches? Ordained ministers, some of whom are from other countries, are valued.  The President of the region, Jan-Albert Roetman, comes from the Netherlands and this year, the Moderator, Andrew Rossiter, is from England; vocations are also beginning to increase.   A sound lay-training package is in place with sessions on the historical and political background to the Pentateuch and the Prophets, sessions on Pastoral Theology and on Social Ethics.

In geographical sectors and in districts, local churches are being called to live out their solidarity with one another in spiritual, financial and human terms.  They will seek to make best use of their resources to ensure that the Gospel is proclaimed and heard in today's world.

*Fleur Houston*

*Pray with the Eglise Réformée de France, twinned with the Wessex Synod.*

**Read**   Ephesians 1:3-14

Help us to realise the presence of the spirit of God in creation
and her presence today among us.
Help us to recognise the spirit of God who spoke through the prophets
and continues to be active in the present.
Help us to acknowledge that the spirit of God creates new communities
of people beyond the barriers of differences.
Help us to accept the stimulation and power that the spirit of God provides,
as we walk humbly to rise up against oppression and injustice in society.

May the spirit of God become alive in the hearts and minds of people today.
May the spirit of God nourish in us new life in Christ.
May the spirit of God guide us to be a witnessing and serving community.
May the spirit of God hold all things together
to become the community of creation.
May the spirit deepen our understanding of truth in Jesus Christ.

Let the spirit of God, giver of life, move us
to call for fullness of life and human dignity.
Let the spirit of God break down the barriers,
and open the path to walk across borders.
Let the spirit of God bring about a new unity of all Christians.
Let the spirit of God relate people to people,
and the whole creation to God in Trinity.

## Here am I *(Luke 1:38)*

Three women, Eva and Francesca French, and Mildred Cable had worked for many years in the early part of the 20th century with the China Inland Mission at Hwochow in the Shansi province. By the time they had reached their fifties, they felt they had done their work, having helped to establish churches and schools. It was now time for Chinese Christians to lead.

But where was God calling them?
After much prayer and heart searching, the answer was given. Together they were called to one of the most desolate places in the world – the Gobi desert. In October 1924 they set up a base at Suchow, 20 miles from the Great Wall of China, and from there set out on numerous expeditions into Outer Mongolia and Chinese Turkistan.

The Bible Societies in Shanghai and London supplied them with scriptures in the diverse languages of the trade routes; and they travelled with these, and all they needed for their journey, packed in a two-wheeled cart. They attended fairs, where they preached and sold their Bibles and tracts. They administered physical and spiritual healing in harems and opium dens. They met White Russian refugees fleeing the revolution, exiles hiding from justice, and a Tibetan monk who had dreamed of Jesus. In these later years, their work continued against a background of civil disturbance, facing warlords and violent soldiers. They learned how to deal with tricky carters and those who planned to rob or attack them. In all of this God met them in their need, and enabled them to go on ministering. Eventually they returned to England in 1936, and worked for the Bible Society, conveying their passion for sharing the scriptures.

*Pray for all those who are asking what God wants them to do with their lives, and where he is calling them.*

**Read** 2 Samuel 7:1-14a; Psalm 89:20-37; Ephesians 2:11-22;
Mark 6:30-34, 53-56

The Lord is God, who keeps faith with all people.
The Lord is God, who holds to the promise made to each one.
The Lord is God, who binds up the broken with cords of compassion.
The Lord is God, who gives access to all and denies none.

You are our God, who disregards
　　　　　the walls of our own making,
　　　　　the barriers of our choosing,
　　　　　the weaknesses in our own fidelity.

Not confined by walls of our own making,
nor accepting the barriers of our choosing,
Jesus, you have broken down all division.
There is no longer a group that is in and a group that is out,
a group that is lost and a group that is home and dry,
no longer a group that can have you and a group that cannot.

You will always put yourself out,
　　　　　to say to those who have no hope,
　　　　　　　　　　who feel outside,
　　　　　　　　　　　　shunned,
　　　　　　　　　　　　　discounted,
　　　　　　　　　you count to me.
　　　　　Your company is valued.
I do not write you off.

Within ourselves you do not demand perfection,
but a setting of sight on integrity.
The sinful and righteous within each of us is accepted by you.

Remind us of your generosity,
and your call to go and do likewise.

2 Samuel 11:1-15
Psalm 14
Ephesians 3:14-21
John 6:1-21

## Rooted in love *(Read Ephesians 3:17)*

We believe in Jesus Christ,
crucified, risen and ascended,
who has battled with evil and won.
He has won with the power of his love,
love which is stronger than all the evil and violence in the world.
We believe in the power on his love,
power alive in his people today,
power to overcome fear and suspicion.
And we put our trust in his love alone
and we turn away from all weapons
that kill our innocent brothers and sisters.
For we cannot rely on the weapons of this world
when all our security, hope and life is in Jesus.
We believe in the power of the risen Christ,
for only he can give us inner security.
And we turn away from the evil of weapons of mass destruction,
of arming ourselves whilst others starve,
of trusting the weapons of evil
to safeguard the true and the good.
We believe in Jesus Christ:
and we trust his power of love and nothing else.

*British Council of Churches 'Mannafest', 1981*

*Pray with the Hong Kong Council of the Church of Christ in China (CWM East Asia Region). We also remember 'Window on the World', CWM European Region's holiday conference at Llangrannog in Wales from 31st July-6th August.*

# True power

**Read**  2 Samuel 11:1-15; Ephesians 3:14-21; John 6:1-21

Almighty God,
yours is the kingdom, the power and the glory.
But *we* have power, too.
Forgive us when we misuse, or diminish it,
or fail to live in your strength.

You set before us the example of King David.
A boy to conquer giants; a king to fulfil your purposes –
but not when power led to lust, lust to lies, lies to lawlessness:
corrupting absolutely the power that was his.
Still people are bullied and brought down by those in high places.
Forgive us if we use *our* power to hide our sin and gain the advantage.
But forgive us, also, for treating our leaders as fair game –
easy targets, to cover our own shortcomings.

You set before us the example of Jesus,
who, empowered by you, fed the crowds and walked the waves.
Forgive us for putting ourselves down, and him on a pedestal.
Remind us that when they tried to make him king
he refused the power that corrupts, and turned to you.
And remind us that he came to show us that *we* can do great things:
share the gifts we have and watch them grow;
weather the storms of life and tread uncertain paths;
rise above our helplessness but not above the law;
be our best for you, and in you find our worth.

You set before us the example of St Paul,
whose power you redirected for your purposes,
and who prayed on his knees for his people to be strengthened
by the power of your Spirit in their hearts.
May we, with them, have the power to comprehend the love of Christ,
to know his power within us, and to give him the glory.

## The fight for justice and dignity

Jyotsna Chatterji, who heads the Joint Women's Programme of the Church of North India, has highlighted government apathy over trafficking in women and girls, and called churches to act. She said: 'Trafficking in narcotics and arms gets much attention from the government. But trafficking in girls and women is not yet a major concern'. She pointed out that the existing Immoral Traffic Prevention Act criminalises only the women victims of trafficking and that the law is not used against clients, pimps and brothel owners who keep women and girls in slavery after having lured them into cities with the promise of jobs. The present government rescue operation – conducting raids in red-light areas and herding out the women to remedial homes – is meaningless, she said. Churches should run rehabilitation programmes to liberate the trafficked women from sexual slavery. She made the comments at a workshop on human trafficking organised by the Commission on Polity and National Governance of National Council of Churches in India

In Botswana Revd Malebogo Mothibi and Revd Cheryl Dibeela are seeking to resist moves to have prostitution legalised. They believe that efforts should be made to help prostitutes earn a living in different ways. Cheryl Dibeela said: 'I do not think it is morally right to legalise sex work, and I am currently trying to help women who had considered prostitution get onto a sewing course, on order to make a living in a different way'.

In Zambia, two missionary doctors at the Mwandi hospital of the United Church of Zambia are seeking to reduce the number of deaths related to reproductive health problems by helping women become more self-reliant. Many poorly educated and financially dependent women marry young, become pregnant, and develop complications. Because of their poverty they cannot afford medical care. The doctors encourage women to develop a business and teach them about health issues, including the dangers of early pregnancy. They also gather women together for discussions about Christianity, including subjects like modesty, hospitality and relationships.

*Pray for all women subjected to degrading or abusive relationships.*

## Read 2 Samuel 11:2-12:13a; Psalm 51:1-12

**David** – Boy's Own hero, war leader, chosen of God;
        but fatally flawed by his arrogant misuse of power.

Loving God, we pray for the men who are as powerful today:
    those elected to high office and those who advise them
    those who hold the top jobs in industry and commerce
    those who are worth many millions
    those who are used to getting what they want.

We also remember the men who expect to get their own way
in their smaller sphere of influence:
    husbands and fathers who resort to violence
    bosses who shout and bully their staff
    those who act without consideration for anyone else.

Confront them with their sin and bring them to repentance.
Create a pure heart within them; give them a new and steadfast spirit.

**Bathsheba** – beautiful enough to attract the attention of a king;
        but without choice, both subject and object.

Loving God, we pray for the women who are as powerless today:
    those forced by culture and religion into traditional marriages
    those treated like slaves in sweat-shops and factories
    those infected with HIV/AIDS by uncaring partners
    those tricked into the sex trade
    those who live in unhappy marriages, abused and bullied
    those used as objects of gratification and then abandoned.
    those who receive unwelcome and lustful looks.

Grant that they may hear the sounds of joy and gladness,
restore in them all that has been broken and hurt;
give them a new and steadfast spirit.

## Give us this day

**Bread of Life, we hunger for you,
we need your truth, we need to change.
We look for you, Jesus.**

Remind us that our own thriving depends
on giving and receiving food that endures.
Plant in us seeds of longing which can be nurtured
and bring to fruit all that promotes unity and real peace.

Remove from us all food that perishes and cannot last,
all that would diminish and destroy us and others.
Gift in us your daily bread which grows and multiplies
and gives the life of heaven to the world.
In your grace, give us this bread always.

Bread of Life, we come to you,
fill us again and again, satisfy our hunger,
fuel our faith, quench our thirst.
Then may we speak the truth in love
and grow up in every way into your likeness.

O God, cleanse our hearts, renew us in right relationships,
never allow us to be greedy and grasping,
so the poor become even poorer.
May we reflect the shalom of your presence,
as your Spirit within gives light and truth, food for our souls.
We pray we may live in the strength of this same Spirit,
willing to become the people you created us to be.

**Bread of life, we hunger for you,
we need your truth, we need to change.
We look for you, Jesus, and thank you for this gift of life.**

*Deborah McVey*

*Pray with the Congregational Union of New Zealand (CWM Pacific Region).*

# Life-giving bread

## Read    John 6:35

Lord, you said that you are bread.
But bread is plain and ordinary,
part of everyday life.
Bread is not special!
It is something that we eat every day.

Yet, Lord, when we are hungry,
bread is easy to reach.
It is satisfying and always ready.
Bread is adaptable, and complete in itself.

Is that what you meant, Lord?
That when we hunger for a spiritual life,
you are easy to reach,
and always ready to satisfy us?

Lord, we thank you that you do come to us
in ways that we can understand.
Thank you for filling us with good things,
so that we can empty ourselves for others.
Thank you for offering us hope and life
through your giving of yourself.

Now may we also be bread for the world.
Nourished by your love and sacrifice,
make us truly live to your glory.

## The smaller beatitudes

Blessed are those who can laugh at themselves; they will have no end of fun.

Blessed are those who can tell a mountain from a molehill; they will be saved a lot of bother.

Blessed are those who know how to relax without looking for excuses; they are on the way to becoming wise.

Blessed are those who know when to be quiet and listen; they will learn a lot of new things.

Blessed are those who are sane enough not to take themselves too seriously; they will be valued by those around them.

Happy are you if you can take small things seriously and face serious things calmly; you will go far in life.

Happy are you if you can appreciate a smile and forget a frown; you will walk on the sunny side of the street.

Happy are you if you can be kind in understanding the attitudes of others; you may be taken for a fool, but this is the price of charity.

Happy are you if you know when to hold your tongue and smile; the Gospel has begun to seep into your heart.

Blessed are they who think before acting and pray before thinking; they avoid many blunders.

Above all,

Blessed are those who recognise the Lord is in all whom they meet; the light of truth shines in their lives: they have found true wisdom.

*Pray with the Ekalesia Kelisiano Tuvalu, one of the smallest of our CWM partners (CWM Pacific Region).*

# O grant us thy wisdom!

**Read** I Kings 2:10-12, 3:3-14; Psalm 111

God of Eternal Wisdom,
we bring before you our corrupt human minds,
with desires of riches and long life, that binds
our souls, our hearts, and keep us all chained.
We plead for liberation for all humankind.

From bondage of sins of lust and of greed;
from our bondage to doctrine and creed.
So we may explore, and experience your vastness
in daily life's chores.

Your blessings have humbled our ancestors.
In love and wisdom
they walked before you in righteousness and faith.

We seek for *our* palate, such wisdom's tasters.

O Grant us your wisdom, so we may discern
the purpose of life and your ways to govern.
'The fear of the Lord is the beginning of wisdom'.

## Here will my servant be also *(Read John 12:26)*

During the Kwangju democratisation movement in 1980, a new form of theology was articulated in Korea called *Minjung* theology. The Minjung are the least and the marginalized. Minjung churches focus on service to the poor, the economically neglected and the politically oppressed. For the last twenty-five years, these churches have been on the forefront of issues of economic and political justice and in compassionately serving the needs of the least.

One such church is Hae-In Church, in Incheon on the coast west of Seoul. Hae-In means 'Liberation of Humans'. The doors are adorned with brightly coloured figures. To get to the church, one climbs stairs, past a landing full of children's shoes, to the 2nd floor, which contains a large open room, kitchen and offices. From that site, hungry elderly people are fed each day, the homeless and jobless are advised, and work to help survivors of domestic violence is organized. The church's pastor Revd Joon-Mo Lee and his wife, who is also ordained, work with a staff of a handful of others. Among their ministries is the provision of a recycling centre, employing homeless men to fix and repair things then made available for sale in a huge warehouse; the provision of housing for people unable to support themselves; a child care centre for working parents; and other outreach efforts to pull people away from addiction and abuse.

Worship takes place on the third floor and all the people served by the church are invited and encouraged to attend, which makes for a very interesting congregation. The pastor and his wife and team aspire to create a worshipping community that works and lives together with the *minjung*. Worship differs from that experienced in most mainline Presbyterian churches. Rather than American and British hymns translated into Korean, accompanied by organ or piano, Hae-In's worship reflects its cultural context: traditional drums are used to accompany Korean songs, and liturgies reflect the commitment of God reaching into the struggles of the people.

Hae-In was a church that almost died 15 years ago. Then the Lees came. The way they tell it, their ministries simply developed in response to listening to the needs of the people around them and responding ..
'one thing led to another', they say.

*Carla Grosch-Miller*

*Pray with the Presbyterian Church of Korea, twinned with the South Western Synod.*

**Read** 1 Kings 8:(1,6,10-11), 22-30; John 6:56-69

Ineffable light

Adored
Mystery

Wind which blows where it chooses
Heavenly home
Only You

Inspire

Animate
Me

Source of Life and Breath,
you choose to dwell on earth,
coming into hearts willing to receive you.
From our first *yes*,
you have marked us with your name.
We cannot be true to it
except by your power and your grace.
Therefore, heed our prayer.
Give us the life you have for us.
Forgive us when we fall short.
And grant us a steadfast faith,
that we may not turn back in the face of difficulty,
but rather be strengthened for the tasks at hand.

## God loves a cheerful giver *(Read 2 Corinthians 9:7)*

Ghana is a place of generous hospitality. The Presbyterian congregations of that country are confident that they will grow. Not for them the wondering whether God will keep the promise that the people of God will be blessed. Despite, or perhaps because of, their relative poverty, they count their blessings and give thanks to God for all that they have.

This is evident in any act of worship, which might be as short as 2 ½ hours or last as long as 5 ½ hours. At some point there will be dancing! The offertory is not the embarrassed or agonising wrestling over what the minimum might be which so often characterises English congregations. The offertory is literally the offering by the congregation of what they have to God. The whole congregation comes out, conga style, to place their money in the basket. What makes this the more remarkable is not the amount but the look of joy in the faces of the dancers. Throughout the country land is being cleared, foundations laid and the bricks made to expand the work of the church. Yes, around Mampong in the Sekyere Presbytery, they do make the bricks by hand! Car journeys are interesting and the prayer of thanksgiving for safe arrival more than routine. The ritual of hospitality includes water for the visitor and the invitation to tell her story. 'Where have you travelled from? And why are you here?' are questions that gently probe the nature of our journeying. For the congregations in Ghana that I visited, that was about having confidence in God and the courage to travel lightly and joyfully. The visitor is left wondering how well we in the UK offer hospitality to the stranger, and deeply challenged to know better the nature and the purpose of our pilgrimage of faith.

*David Grosch-Miller*

*Pray with the Presbyterian Church in Ghana.*

# Self-sufficient or God-dependent?

**Read** Mark 7:8

Forgive us, Father God,
for we have created your church
in the image that we want,
and have hemmed ourselves in
with dogma and doctrine,
committees and words.
We have turned your Word
into a means to an end,
and have failed to act with sense and compassion.

Forgive us, Father God,
we believe that we are your people
but we have become static,
failing to move with the times.
We cling to the past
instead of running to embrace the future.
We praise with our lips, but our hearts are cold.
We have used our buildings as our prisons,
instead of making them into community centres.

Forgive us, Father God,
we are so self sufficient
that we forget to be God-dependent.
We are so sure that we are right,
that we forget to contemplate being wrong.
Give us a new vision
of what it means to be your children,
not chained and bound, but gloriously freed from the past
to serve the world in the present and so praise you.

## Racial Justice Sunday

We believe that the universe was created by a loving God, who chose to become a human being in Jesus Christ, who has redeemed the world, and sent the Holy Spirit to enable us to love one another with God's love. All human beings are equally children of God and loved by God. Since none is outside the love of God, none should be outside our love either. We believe that the diversity of the human race was no mistake on God's part. God deliberately created variety within the human family and wants us to take as much delight in that variety as God does.

But racism persists in Britain and Ireland. At its most obvious and brutal, it takes the form of physical attacks, which sometimes end in murder. It takes other forms as well, like discrimination within the police force, popular prejudice against Travellers or people seeking asylum, or reluctance to accept people of a different ethnic or cultural group as neighbours. Even within the churches, people can face discrimination and unkindness because they are different from the majority in a particular community.

As people of faith, the defeat of racism is the business of us all. For it is only through the active participation of the many, that justice is done, and true liberation of those that are oppressed secured.

For example, through the Bail Circle of the Churches Council for Racial Justice, destitute individuals and families fleeing either political persecution or institutionally-imposed hardship, and detained in our prisons or detention centres without support, are offered a modicum of relief through the sacrificial generosity of those volunteering to stand bail for them.

When we stand for justice, even by observing Racial Justice Sunday, we are not only following Nelson Mandela's bidding to 'liberate others', but making visible God's will for love, truth and justice.

> "The worth of an individual does not lie in the measure of his intellect, his racial origin, or his social position … An individual has value because he has value to God". *(Martin Luther King Jr.)*

*Pray for all victims of racism, and for the success of all attempts to fight it.*

**Read** James 2:14-17

God of love and mercy, infinite, and active,
help us to have the faith that works for the betterment of others.
Help us to show our faith in action to establish justice.
Help us to respect and learn from others who are different from us.
Help us to move away from our assumptions and prejudices,
to work for bringing new possibilities in our thinking and doing.
Help us be liberated from our personal and cultural prejudices,
so that we can work for peace and unity.
Help us to extend ourselves into life affirming ways
of reconciliation and healing.
Help us to be united in the spirit without losing our identities.
Help us to realise that the strength of the church
lies in the diversity of its members.
We give thanks for the diversity of membership in our churches.

**Blessed are those who respect and trust
those who are different from themselves.
Blessed are those who reflect God's compassion with their neighbours.
Blessed are those who do justice, love kindness, walk humbly with God.**

**The heart of the matter** *(Read Hebrews 9: 24-28; Mark 12: 38-44)*

Sacrifice is not an easy word, Lord.

Implied within it are burning, searing, spilling, dying,
hurt, cost, loss and pain.

Not a nice word.
Not one to like.
Not one to seek after.

Yet you call us to it.
You say follow me.
You who gave up all you are and all you had, say follow me,
not sacrificing others, but sacrificing self.

But we say, it is too much, it is too hard.
I can do this little bit       – only if the world knows
                               – only if the world honours
                               – only if the world counts it
                               – only if the difference it makes is clear
and we can say 'Yes, that was me!'
This you neither promise nor desire.
Your concern is for the attitude of heart
and not the action or its outcome.

You do say, however, that in our poverty and pain,
when your love in us makes us generous
and no-one else either notices or cares,
that you will see the hidden cost
of what we give and offer,
proclaim it good and worthy
and rejoice.

*Helen Pope*

*Pray with the Presbyterian Church of Myanmar (CWM East Asia Region).*

Lord, my God,
my Saviour, my All,
my One, True God,
Christ of my heart,
my soul's redeemer.

I call you this, for this you are.
The earth, the skies,
all creation tells me.
How can I neither see nor hear
your greatness, glory, beauty, perfection?
How can I refrain to name you as you are?

How can I choose any other than you?
What more could I desire?
Who better could I seek?

There is more to finding you than fellowship
and more to worship than my words.

For worship is
praise,
and a walking in your way,
following you
on the obedient path.
Worship is as much of sacrifice and service,
as the experience of revelation and of fire.

I love you and know your worth.

It is not enough to worship with my lips,
I must follow with my feet.

## Contrast and conflict *(Read James 3:13-4:3)*

Jamaica is famous as a holiday island of sun, sea and swaying palms. But for the visitor prepared to look deeper than the snap-shots of the all-inclusive holiday, for those willing to travel further than the tourist who remains within the grounds and beach of the luxurious hotel, the reality of Jamaica is even more rich and colourful than its flourishing and vibrant vegetation. Jamaica is a land of enormous contrast, of bewildering extremes.

A huge number of radiant, dedicated Christians inhabit this island which is reputed to be home to more churches per square mile than anywhere else in the world, Christians whole-heartedly committed in their service to God.

Yet co-existing with this evidence of deep-rooted goodness, a real evil stalks the land. People speak of corruption in politics, of drug barons and gun-related killings. Violence and a frightening incidence of road accidents make life fragile, even cheap, rendering all the more poignant the oft-repeated call to worship: 'This is the day that the Lord has made; let us rejoice and be glad in it' *(Psalm 118:24)*.

The discerning will use their eyes to see and admire the grandeur of Devon House in Kingston, built by the first black millionaire in the 1870s, a symbol of emancipation and hope; yet they will also use their ears to hear and empathise with the near-hopelessness of too many young men who are unemployed 125 years later. The sight of the spacious mansions of the wealthy in Uptown Kingston, when juxtaposed alongside the zinc roofs and graffiti-riddled walls of the cramped garrisons in Downtown Kingston, is unsettling to the point of being heart-rending.

Wealth and poverty, hope and despair, beauty and ugliness, life and death, even heaven and hell, such are the symbiotic twins of Jamaica, land of contrast. So in one small island we find concentrated the painful paradoxes of our contemporary world.

*Gillian Heald, who did a student placement in Jamaica in 2004*

*Pray with the United Church in Jamaica and the Cayman Islands (CWM Caribbean Region).*

# An unlikely bride

**Read**    Mark 9:30-37; Psalm 1; Proverbs 31:10-31

Son of Man, let us walk with you.
You are too good for this world, too transparent, too courageous –
a Saviour without sin travelling to a holy city.
You will be crucified again.  So will your holy city.
But you are all we have.  You are all that makes sense.
So let us walk with you.

We, too, are threatened by perfection.
We struggle with the scriptures we revere.
The Psalms begin with the Lord watching over the righteous
while the ways of the wicked perish.
Where does that leave us, who fall somewhere in between?
The Proverbs end with a hymn to a perfect wife,
constant and competent, prepared for the morrow,
devoted to her husband, the needy and God,
with never a thought for herself.
But how does that help us?  Who could ever measure up to her?
Only you, Son of Man.
For you stand alone.  And alone you remain.
Your only bride is the Church.

Son of Humanity, you do not offer your perfection, but your love.
Let us walk with you, then: your human church, your unworthy bride.
Like the first ones.  Faithless and flawed and full of possibility.
Vying for greatness.  Scared of the future.  Guilty of betrayal.
The ways of the righteous and wicked mixed inseparably in us all.

We do not know why you choose us or what you see in us.
Beauty must be in the eye of the beholder.
But make us worthy partners, not through our greatness but your love.
Help us to live more for you and others, less for ourselves.
And wherever you take us, let us walk with you.

## Rags to riches to rags

At midnight on 31 December 2004 the World Trade Organisation scrapped the main quota system that governs the global clothing and textile trade – the Multi-Fibre Agreement – ending 30 years of protection for one of the developing world's most vulnerable industries. Across the world as many as 27 million people might be thrown out of work, but Bangladesh is likely to be one country most affected. Sales of garments and textiles to the US and EU accounted for 84% of all the country's exports in 2000, contributing 80% of its hard currency earnings. The UN predicts that 1 to 1.5 million people will loose their jobs – the majority of whom are women.

Already the effects are being felt. Twenty-year-old Farida used to work as a machine operator making trousers and shirts, earning £22 a month. But because there are so few orders for the factory she has lost her job, and now she works in a factory sorting scraps of cloth by colour but earning only £10 a month – not enough to live on.

The garment industry has given thousands of women the chance to work, but also levels of self-reliance and confidence as well as a way of clawing their way out of extreme poverty. Salma Ali, the executive director of the Bangladesh National Women's Lawyers Association told Christian Aid: 'These women will have very few choices. They are used to city life and don't want to go back to the villages where there is no electricity or running water. Many of them are single … some will be able to migrate and get a good job, others will be the victims of trafficking'.

*(see: www.christianaid.org.uk/indepth/412rags/index.htm)*

But for others there is still hope. Shafili Begum wanted to set up a small fish rearing business, and she was offered a loan from a credit scheme supported by the Christian Commission for Development in Bangladesh (CCDB). Since then she has earned an income four times greater than the original investment, and the surplus fish provide a healthy supplement to the family diet.

*Pray for the Christian Commission for Development in Bangladesh, one of our Commitment for Life partners.*

**Read** Esther 7:1-6, 9-10, 9:20-22; Psalm 124; James 5:13-20; Mark 9:38-50

We pray for people, places and times of total overwhelming,
when the raging waters of human disaster seem to swallow us alive,
when life comes to a full-stop and all that is familiar has all but gone.
**Our help is in the name of GOD who made heaven and earth.**

*Let my life be given me – that is my petition –
and the lives of my people – that is my request. (Esther 7:3b)*

We pray for those who feel abandoned in one way or another,
through ill-health or sickness or the loss of one beloved to them,
and for those who feel there can be no escape from their situation.
**Our help is in the name of GOD who made heaven and earth.**

*Whoever gives you a cup of water to drink because you bear the name
of Christ will by no means lose the reward. (Mark 9:41)*

We pray for all who cannot articulate their particular need,
who do not know what they want or have no interest in life,
all who are lonely and without assurance of love and care.
**Our help is in the name of GOD who made heaven and earth.**

*Turn sorrow into gladness and mourning into a holiday,
make days of feasting, days for sending gifts of food to one another
and presents for the poor. (Esther 9:22)*

We pray for ourselves, in times of trouble and suffering,
when in feebleness we can barely cry out to you.
May the prayers of our companions in Christ raise us up.
**Our help is in the name of GOD who made heaven and earth.**

## Let the children come to me

Children living in a slum in Kolkata (Calcutta) in India are getting primary school education from a club-school set up by the Church of North India (CNI). 26 children attend the school started by St John's Diocesan girls higher secondary school. The students, aged 6 to 14, receive textbooks, notebooks, bags and pens, and a daily meal. The school was set up after St John's teachers discovered that 99% of children have never attended school.

5 street children in Delhi have set up small businesses after getting a loan from a CNI rescue and rehabilitation project. They have started a peanut stall, a tea shop, and a stall selling freshly cooked boiled eggs and omelettes. The boys are doing well enough to repay the loan regularly every week. The CNI, through the Delhi Brotherhood Society, works to improve the lives of street children by providing them with shelter, education, medical care and pastoral support.

The Church of South India Bishop Sargent School is educating and training mentally disabled children so that they can take part in society. Children with learning difficulties are often isolated and neglected in Indian society. Parents hide them away because they are considered a sign of God's punishment. The philosophy here, however, is that these children are accepted as God's children, and special education is provided for them. Some pupils are trained in tailoring, baking, handicrafts, sales and agriculture. There are 130 children in the school with a waiting list of 800. It places 40% of children in society, 30% to be employable in sheltered workshops, and 30% need life-long care.

*Pray with the Church of North India (CWM South Asia Region).*

**Read**    Mark 10:13-16

How can we enter the kingdom of God?
Now that's a question indeed.

Jesus said we had to become like little children first.
A 98 year-old once asked me what he meant by that.

Is it that we need the spirit of wide-eyed wonder,
prepared to give thanks and glory to God for everyday miracles,
like the song of the robin, or raindrops on the washing line,
like the first feel of sand, or reflections in a puddle?

Or could it be he meant the quality of childlike innocence,
ready to accept new friends with no prejudice or suspicion,
showing unveiled anger and joy, speaking with transparent truth?

Was it their lack of foresight Jesus recognised,
a child's ability to live for the moment, not afraid of the future,
eager to take new steps because the world is there to be explored?

Loving God, guide us to know what it is about childhood
that is the key to living in your kingdom.
For it might be all or none of these things.
Maybe it is just that children are inescapably dependent,
totally and absolutely, on their parents.
If so, Lord, we ask that you take from us all that gets in the way
of our recognition of your sustaining love:
    all self-sufficiency, which means we deny we need you,
    all pride, which places us at the centre of the universe.
Help us to turn to you, to know your everlasting arms beneath us,
your hand of blessing above us,
and if we are thrown into the air, to trust that you will catch us.

## The future beckons

The Church of Lippe is a united Lutheran and Reformed church made up of 71 parishes and 200,000 members, and with 145 ministers.

The Church has a colourful worship and parish life, boasting 50 church choirs and 62 brass bands. It provides a family education service; a women's department; youth services; and diaconal welfare work among the elderly, young children and refugees. International partnerships are maintained with churches in Hungary, Togo, Poland, Nepal, Romania, Ghana, Lithuania, Indonesia and South Africa. There is a strong emphasis on Justice, Peace and the Integrity of Creation.

Like other European churches, the Church of Lippe is at a crossroads, and the second part of their mission statement reflects this:

> We are children of a great promise.
> > God's Word is alive.
> > God's Holy Spirit gathers people.
> > The future is in God's hand.

> We are a Church on the move …
> > On our journey, we pause to reflect.
> > We know our limitations.
> > But we are also aware of our potential.
> > Great and manifold are the gifts of God.
> > Great and vast is the task of our Church.

Church life changes constantly through listening anew to the Good News entrusted to us and in the response to far-reaching changes: social transformation, demographic development, loss of income, decreasing membership.

We pause to reflect and ask ourselves: what are our strengths and our weaknesses? How could and how should we proceed from here?

*Ray Adams*

*Pray with the Church of Lippe, twinned with the South Western Synod.*

**Read**   Job 23:1-9, 16-17; Psalm 22:1-15

God of Eternal Joy,
grey skies, blue mood, our complaints are bitter.
We have reasons for seasons of sadness, where is our joy?

God of Light,
vanishing in darkness is what our souls desire.
We are scared of light; the realities of hunger and poverty
are too haunting and daunting for our eyes.

God of our ancestors,
why have you forsaken us?
We need your protection and care in this world.

God, grant us your boldness so that we may
face, confront, and encounter the bitterness that overwhelms.
We trust you as God of past, present and future,
who always delivered, and continues to deliver.

Strengthen us so that even if we do not understand,
yet we play our part, to make this world to stand
for peace and joy, so that you reign
and we get a sense of purpose, and see the vision grand.

## The servanthood of all believers

Concerning the why and how and what and who of ministry,
one image keeps surfacing:
a table that is round.

It will take some sawing to be roundtabled,
some redefining and redesigning.
Such redoing and rebirthing of narrowlong churching
can painful be for people and tables.

It would mean no daising and throning,
for but one King is there, and he was a footwasher,
at table no less.

We must be loved into roundness,
for God has called a People, not 'them' and 'us'.

At one time our narrowlong churches
were built to resemble the cross,
but it does no good for buildings to do so
if lives do not.

Roundtabling means no preferred seating,
no first and last, no better, and no corners
for 'the least of these'.

Roundtabling means room for the Spirit and gifts
and disturbing profound peace for all.

*Chuck Lathrop*

*Pray with the Congregational Federation.*

# Remind us again

**Read** Job 38:1-7, (34-41); Mark 10:35-45

Great and gracious God,

All our words stumble and fall before your might and your majesty.
We speak of that which we do not understand.
We ask for things we cannot apprehend.

Can it be any other way?
We are limited beings,
made in limitless love.

Give us the grace
to wear our ignorance wisely,
to welcome the ground on which we walk,
the air we breathe,
and the life we live
as gifts from your loving hand.

And when our hubris shouts down our humility,
when we seek to bend your will to ours,
remind us again who we are,
dust formed in your image,
with the capacity and the choice
to become servants of the living God.

## What do you want me to do for you?
*(Read Mark 10:46-52)*

Merciful God, we sit here like blind beggars.
Like beggars we've come to receive,
not knowing what the day will bring.

Like beggars, we've come to receive
what we haven't earned in any way, trusting in your mercy alone;
trusting that out of the great store-house of your grace
there will be enough to supply all our needs.

Like blind beggars, we know
how difficult life is when you can't see.
We are particularly blind when it comes to inward things.
We understand so little about the people around us.
We understand so little about our own motives.
So we are always tripping up,
hurting others by our selfishness and insensitivity,
hurting you by our anxiety and irritability …

Like blind beggars, we know
our first and foremost need is to see.
We need forgiving and healing.
We need your light.
We need your individual attention –
to accept us, to touch us, to change us.
And so we want to shout out,
**Jesus, Son of David, have mercy on me.**

Let us today receive our sight
that we may see the glory of your grace
and be able to follow you more closely.

*Pray with the Presbyterian Church in Singapore.*

# My world or yours?

## Pentecost 21

**Read** Job 42:1-6; Hebrews 7:25

My world is a battleground of mistrust and broken promises;
your world is a haven of faith and covenant.
My world is a world of artificial barriers;
your world is a place of open gates and opportunity.
My world is one of defensive mechanisms;
your world is a rainbow of hope and love.

Lord, I find it hard to yield completely to your will,
and not to build barriers and defences that keep you out,
or seek reasons for what goes wrong within it
or to understand your plans for me.
I find it hard not to immerse myself in worldly things.

Lord, help me to yield to you,
to surrender my life, my hope, my fears
into your hands, for to resist is to die,
and to yield to you is to gain abundant life.

In your hands I could become
hopeful, and bring hope to those around me,
for the cross of Jesus
smashes every barrier down,
breaches every barricade
and makes the whole world worthy
of his sacrifice.

## Doing the Lord's work *(Read Psalm 146)*

In the Ukrainian city of Munkas, an American Baptist missionary was updating his apartment as he and his wife were expecting their first baby. He had a new bathroom suite fitted and the builders put the old bath in the courtyard ready for disposal. A minister friend living in Nagybereg with his family asked if he could have the old bath, now covered in cement, as it was better than his, and it was duly installed. The Church Elder who fitted the bath for the minister asked if he could have his old bath, as it was better than his, so the 40-year-old bath, very rusty and with the enamel surface almost non-existent was moved to the Elder's house. The bath which it replaced was put out in his garden ready for use as a rainwater tank, but someone took it during the night, no doubt because, although it was holed, it was 'better than his'.

Such experiences are not uncommon in Carpathia, where the unemployment situation is desperate; where teachers earn £15, and tractor drivers £5, a month, but where a second-hand tractor still costs £2000.

The Reformed Church cares for its congregations not only spiritually, but practically as well. The United Reformed Church has been able to help financially, providing money to rebuild churches, helping to fund Christian schools and supporting the work with gypsies. Also help has been given to families where the men have had to go to Hungary to find work, leaving women and children for months at a time without any means of support. Newly ordained pastors are now placed in villages, usually looking after more than one congregation, which can number 500-700 people. Their living conditions are often as basic as their church members. Most people in the region live on what they produce in their own gardens. In towns, many flat-dwellers depend on the relatives in country areas for food. Street children, abandoned because their parents cannot support them, are a growing concern to the Reformed Church.

*Pray with the Reformed Church of Carpathia (part of the Hungarian Reformed Church), twinned with the Southern Synod.*

**Read**    Mark 12: 28-34; Ruth 1:1-18

Lord, you teach us to
love our neighbour as ourselves;
> the neighbour of another faith,
> the neighbour of another culture,
> the neighbour of another race,
> the neighbour of another language.

Help us to show the gift of honesty to our neighbours.
Help us to show the gift of charity to our neighbours.
Help us to show the gift of dignity to our neighbours.
Help us to show the gift of love to our neighbours.

Loving God, make our heart to love our neighbours, and make us
tolerant towards people who have contrary views.

Let your power provide inspiration for the quest for truth,
the struggle against injustice, and the longing for new communities
that brings all people together.

Your love is for all people; you bring life, hope and salvation to all.
Let our unselfishness be shown in love, so that we may able to say
to our neighbours, 'your people are my people'.

## REMEMBRANCE SUNDAY
### A Widow's Tale  *(Read the book of Ruth)*

As she looked into her grandchild's eyes and gently held his tiny fingers her mind went back to the night it had all begun. It seemed so long ago and yet it wasn't really.

*It had been a warm night and yet she couldn't stop shivering; the stars were out but she could not see them through the veil of tears that coursed down her face. It was the end of everything. They had travelled so far, scraped a meagre existence in the hope of a brighter future but now the dream was over and she was alone – her husband and two sons cruelly taken from her. She was a stranger in a strange land. Her daughters-in law would remarry into new families and she would be alone. There would be no grandchildren now.*

*She had returned to her hometown, a defeated woman dependent on the goodwill of friends; a faceless woman in a society that had no place for widows. What was she to do?*
*What hope was there? But, she had not returned alone, surprisingly her daughter-in-law Ruth, had travelled with her. She had not expected that, and while she had wallowed in her own self-pity, Ruth had quietly gone about finding them food. As time had gone by she had begun to take an interest again, and been amazed to discover who had helped Ruth – none other than her husband's cousin! Even then she could not have foreseen the unexpected course that events would follow, it had been nothing less than a miracle.*

The child stirred in her arms and she held him close. He was special, very special and who knew what might happen next. She had a family again, a grandchild, and perhaps there would be great-grandchildren and more, all from this very special baby, her hope for the future.

*Heather Whyte*

*Pray for all suffering the trauma of war and violence at the present time.*

**Read** Ruth 3:1-5, 4:13-17; Mark 12:38-44

Father, on *this* day we pray for those left behind;
for the widows and orphans of conflict and terror.
Help us to remember *them*.

Help us remember they have needs we cannot see.
They have lost everything
as their loved ones have given everything.
Their dreams are shattered; they need
care while time and space
      allows the dust of their dreams to settle;
help to pick up the remaining fragments
      and piece together a new future;
and hope: you are that hope,
      for you too have lost a loved one.

Give us wisdom and inspiration
to provide for their unseen needs.
Through our human love
may they find your holy grace.

As we remember, we pray for peace
      through justice and equal sharing;
      through wisdom and humility in those
      to whom the world has given power;
      through the end of conflict
      and the dawning of your kingdom.
Father, we pray for light in our darkness,
the light that sparkled in a baby's eyes
as you blessed the world with your presence.

Help us remember.

1 Samuel 1:4-20
1 Samuel 2:1-10
Hebrews 10:11-4 (15-18), 19-25
Mark 13:1-8

## Watering the seed

The Dabane Trust in Zimbabwe provides cheap sustainable water supplies, such as dams and water tanks, for communities to increase their agricultural production and provide water for their families and their animals. The organisation specialises in water abstraction, where water is pumped by hand from water-bearing sand into tanks. The project demands a great deal of community involvement, with many women market gardeners making a considerable input to their family income. Many of them are the sole bread-winners in the family, as their husbands are working away or are too ill or old to work. They are managing to put their children through school with profits from the vegetables that they sell.

Beritha Moyo grows onions, carrots, green vegetables, pumpkins and groundnuts in her vegetable garden. She used to be dependent on arable crops such as maize, groundnuts, or sorghum. 'Last year was a total write off. That's why the vegetable garden is so important for us. We can always be assured of a certain harvest. We know we're always going to get water here'. Beritha grows enough from her vegetable garden for the family and other relatives. She sells the rest and with the profits from the vegetables she has been able to pay school fees for her son Mduduzi. "I also bought plates and blankets for the house, and paid for my husband's medical fees. Before, the only vegetable that we ate was okra, day in, day out. Now we are definitely healthier". With help from the Dabane Trust, she learnt how to record all her outgoing and incoming expenses. 'Now I always ensure that I make a profit because I know how much I have spent on inputs such as seeds. I've also done practical training in agricultural techniques such as how to prepare a seed bed, how to transplant crops and the importance of crop rotation. I also took part in leadership training and we learnt about what different roles in committees entail'.

*Pray for the Dabane Trust in Zimbabwe, one of our Commitment for Life partners.*

**Read** 1 Samuel 1:14-20, 2:1-10; Mark 13:1-8

As the last leaves fall and the nights close in,
and the first signs of winter chill the air,
awaken in us, living God,
the urge to look beyond and yearn for the light.

As the waiting time approaches
when nature migrates and hibernates
and becomes dormant in barren ground,
keep alive the seeds of hope that know their time will come.

And in the meantime let us stand with Hannah as she prays,
and with all who have waited too long, watching their time slip by,
their prayers unanswered, at least as they had hoped;
their justice still denied, their longing hard to bear.

And give us their defiance to live against the evidence.
'The poor are always with us' – and yet they work for justice.
'Always wars and rumours' – and still they pray for peace.
Without such prayer and heartbreak
the world might just give in, and lose its soul.

And in this mean time, let us stay with them:
facing pain that someday could be birth pangs,
hunting beneath the fallen leaves for signs of life,
searching amongst the scattered stones of once proud temples.

And with every discovery, every little conquest,
every piece of good news unreported,
let us celebrate the in-break of your kingdom.
Hannah's hymn of praise!  First Magnificat!  Final restoration!
And let us share what you have given, the harvest of our longings,
offered back in gratitude for the healing of the nations.

## A Nicaraguan Lord's Prayer

Don't say 'Father' if you don't behave like his child each day.
Don't say 'Our' if you only ever think about yourself.
**Our Father, who art in heaven**.
Don't say 'Hallowed be your name' if you don't honour that name.
Don't say 'Your Kingdom come' if you are weighed down with material goods.
**Hallowed be your name, Your Kingdom come**.
Don't say 'Your will be done' if you don't accept the hard times.
Don't say ' As it is in heaven' if you only ever think of earthly matters.
**Your will be done, on earth as it is in heaven**.
Don't say 'Our daily bread' if you have no concern for the hungry or the sick.
**Give us this day our daily bread**
Don't say 'Forgive us our sins' if you remain angry with your brothers.
**Forgive us our sins, as we forgive those who sin against us.**
Don't say 'Lead us not into temptation' if you intend to continue sinning.
Don't say 'deliver us from evil' if you won't make a stand against injustice.
**Lead us not into temptation, but deliver us from evil.**
Don't say 'Amen' without considering the words of your prayer.
**For the Kingdom, the power and the glory are yours, now and for ever. Amen.**

*Pray with the Guyana Congregational Union (CWM Caribbean Region).*

# Who is, and who was and who is to come

## Pentecost 25
### Christy the King

**Read**   Revelation 1:1:4b-8; John 18:33-37

God who always was, God of the past,
then and there we have praised you;
your kingdom was not from this world.
Your own people handed you over for trial
and you died as a servant king.
You have given us peace, not as the world gives,
but peace that has brought us into this moment.
**We thank you.**

God who always is, God of the present,
here and now we praise you;
your kingdom is not from this world.
We proclaim you Alpha and Omega,
yet we limit you and keep you to ourselves.
Forgive us, great and mighty King of all being
for rejecting your message of peace and joy.
**Forgive us we pray.**

God who is to come, God of the future,
we wonder when and where we will praise you,
your kingdom will not be from this world.
We glimpse its future promise; your forgiveness releases us
from past and present into the unknown and all that lies ahead.
May we crown you in our hearts, breathing the life of your Spirit,
for you we were born and to you we will return when days are done.
**Bless and keep us always in your love.**

# Acknowledgements

Prayers on the right-hand pages in this Handbook are by the following authors:

**Barbara Bennett** - prayers dated 11, 25 December, 12 February, 10 April, 7 May, 18 June, 9 July, 13 August, 3 September, 29 October

**Ken Chippindale** - prayers dated 6 August and 8 October

**Carla Grosch-Miller** - prayers dated 27 November, 4 December, 22 January, 5 February, 19 March, 2 April, 30 April, 2 July, 27 August, 22 October

**Jasmine Jebakani** - prayers dated 18 December, 6 January, 19 February, 11 April, 14 May, 16 July, 10 September, 5 November

**David Jonathan** - prayers dated 29 January, 26 March, 23 April, 4, 25 June, 20 August, 15 October

**Deborah McVey** - prayers dated 15 January, 12 March, 14, 15, 16 April, 11 June, 13 August, 1 October, 26 November

**Helen Pope** - prayers dated 1 January, 26 February, 1 March, 12 April, 21 May, 23 July, 17 September

**Heather Whyte** - prayer dated 12 November

**Brian Woodcock** - prayers dated 8 January, 5 March, 9, 13 April, 25, 28 May, 30 July, 24 September, 19 November

The full list of copyright holders for material on the left-hand pages is available from Communications and Editorial, The United Reformed Church, 86 Tavistock Place, London WC1H 9RT. No material from the Prayer Handbook should be reproduced in any form without reference to that office.

27 November  Paragraphs 1&2: Christian Aid 'Stories for World AIDS Day 2004, used by permission; paragraph 3: CWM 'Inside Out', issue 42 (Oct-Dec 04); paragraphs 4&5: CWM; prayer: Christian Aid Prayer Diary, Dec 04-March 05, used by permission

4 December  David Grosch-Miller

11 December  'Facts on the Ground', Christian Aid Report 2004, used by permission

18 December  Wendy Ross-Barker, used by permission

25 December  'The Light Shines', Christian Aid 1985, used by permission

8 January  Simbarishe Agushito

15 January  Erzsebet Abraham

29 January  The Leprosy Mission New Day magazine, January 2004, www.leprosymission.org.uk

5 February  Fleur Houston

12 February  'Getting Ready', study resource for World Council of Churches 9th Assembly

19 February  'Getting Ready', study resource for World Council of Churches 9th Assembly

5 March  Fairtrade Foundation Website February 2005, used by permission

19 March © Sandy Ryrie, used by permission

2 April  source unknown

9 April  Friends of Sabeel

10, 11, 12, 13 April  Gillian Heald

16 April  Shirley Erena Murray, Copyright © 1992 Hope Publishing
    Company, Administer by CopyCare, PO Box 77, Hailsham BN27 3EF, UK,
    music@copycare.com.  Used by permission

23 April  Christian Aid News, Spring 2005, used by permission

30 April  The Bible Society 'Word in Action', Summer 2004,
    www.biblesociety.org.uk/wordinaction

7 May  Clive Fowle

14 May  Christian Aid News, Spring 2005, used by permission

21 May  © Sandy Ryrie, used by permission

28 May  Malcolm Haslett

4 June  Wendy Ross-Barker, used by permission

11 June  CWM 'Inside Out', issue 40 (June/July 04)

18 June  Barbara Bennett - 'Windows', Easter 2003, used by permission

16 July  Fleur Houston

23 July  The Bible Society 'Word in Action', Winter 2004,
    www.biblesociety.org.uk/wordinaction

30 July  Resource book for the Week of Prayer for Christian Unity 2004, CTBI

20 August  author unknown

3 September  David Grosch-Miller

10 September  Racial Justice Sunday packs 2003 and 2004,
    Churches Commission for Racial Justice, CTBI

24 September  Gillian Heald

15 October  Ray Adams

22 October  Chuck Lathrop - permission sought

29 October  author unknown

5 November  Janet Davidson

26 November  Attributed to Movemiento Communale de Mategalpa,
    Nicaragua, in 'Through the Year with Christian Aid', used by permission


Items from CWM News appear on pages dated 27 November, 1 January,
5 February, 1 March, 26 March, 25 June, 2, 9 July, 6 August, 8 October.
CWM News is a free email news service of the Council for World Mission.
If you would like to receive regular news from partner churches around the
world, contact: news@cwmission.org.uk


Items on the pages for 26 February, 12 March, 1 October, 19 November are
from Commitment for Life materials.